My **revision** notes

Edexcel A-level History

REBELLION AND DISORDER UNDER THE TUDORS

1485–1603

Roger Turvey

Series editor
Peter Callaghan

HODDER
EDUCATION
AN HACHETTE UK COMPANY

Orders: please contact Bookpoint Ltd, 130 Milton Park, Abingdon, Oxon OX14 4SE. Telephone: +44 (0)1235 827720. Fax: +44 (0)1235 400454. Email education@bookpoint. co.uk. Lines are open from 9 a.m. to 5 p.m., Monday to Saturday, with a 24-hour message answering service. You can also order through our website: www.hoddereducation.co.uk.

ISBN: 978 1 4718 7661 5

© Roger Turvey 2017

First published in 2017 by
Hodder Education
An Hachette UK Company
Carmelite House
50 Victoria Embankment
London EC4Y 0DZ
www.hoddereducation.co.uk

Impression number 10 9 8 7 6 5 4 3 2

Year   2020 2019 2018 2017

Cover photo © WawroDesign/Alamy Stock Photo
Illustrations by Integra
Typeset by Integra Software Services Pvt. Ltd., Pondicherry, India
Printed in India

A catalogue record for this title is available from the British Library.

My revision planner

5 Troublesome Ireland: Tyrone's Rebellion, 1594–1603

Part 2 Aspects in breadth: controlling a fractious nation – changes in Tudor government, 1485–1603

Theme 1 Changes in governance at the centre

Theme 2 Gaining the co-operation of the localities

Introduction

About Paper 3

Paper 3 Rebellion and disorder under the Tudors, 1485–1603, combines a depth study of challenges to authority with a broader thematic study of changes in Tudor government. Paper 3 tests you against two Assessment Objectives: AO1 and AO2.

AO1 tests your ability to:
- organise and communicate your own knowledge
- analyse and evaluate key features of the past
- make supported judgements
- deal with concepts of cause, consequence, change, continuity, similarity, difference and significance.

On Paper 1, AO1 tasks require you to write essays from your own knowledge.

AO2 tests your ability to:
- analyse and evaluate source material from the past
- explore the value of source material by considering its historical context.

On Paper 2, the AO2 task requires you to write an essay which analyses two sources which come from the period you have studied.

Paper 3 is worth 30 per cent of your A-level.

Structure

Paper 3 is structured around two themes and five key topics.

The exam is divided into three sections, which relate to different aspects of your course:

Aspect of the course	Exam
1: Challenging the succession, 1485–1499	Section A (AO2) and Section B (AO1)
2: Challenging religious changes, 1533–37	
3: Kett's Rebellion, 1549	
4: The Revolt of the Northern Earls, 1569–70	
5: Tyrone's Rebellion, 1594–1603	
Theme 1: Changes in governance at the centre	Section C (AO1)
Theme 2: Gaining the co-operation of the localities	

The exam

The Paper 3 exam lasts for 2 hours and 15 minutes, and is divided into three sections.

Section A and Section B test the depth of your historical knowledge of the five topics:
- Section A requires you to answer one compulsory question concerning a single source. You should spend 15 to 20 minutes reading the source and planning your answer, and around 35 to 40 minutes writing the essay.
- Section B requires you to write one essay from a choice of two. As this is a depth paper, questions can be set on single events. Section B essays usually test your knowledge of a shorter period than Section C. You should spend 35 to 40 minutes on Section B.
- Section C requires you to answer one question, from a choice of two. Questions in Section C will focus on the two themes. Questions will cover at least 100 years. Questions can focus on either themes, or may test knowledge of both themes. You should spend 35 to 40 minutes on Section C.

How to use this book

This book has been designed to help you to develop the knowledge and skills necessary to succeed in this exam. Each section is made up of a series of topics organised into double-page spreads. On the left-hand page, you will find a summary of the key content you need to learn. Words in bold in the key content are defined in the glossary (pages 107–8). On the right-hand page you will find exam-focused activities. Together, these two strands of the book will take you through the knowledge and skills essential for examination success.

Examination activities

There are three levels of exam-focused activities.
- Band 1 activities are designed to develop the foundational skills needed to pass the exam. These have a green heading and this symbol.
- Band 2 activities are designed to build on the skills developed in Band 1 activities and to help you achieve a C grade. These have an orange heading and this symbol.
- Band 3 activities are designed to enable you to access the highest grades. These have a purple heading and this symbol.

Each section ends with an exam-style question and sample answers with commentary. This should give you guidance on what is required to achieve the top grades.

1 Challenging the succession, 1485–99

Henry Tudor's hold on the throne, 1485–87

REVISED

Background

A nation's government, security and well-being depend on the character and strength of its ruler. This was particularly true during the Middle Ages, when kings had the power to pass laws, raise revenue and make war. Richard III's seizure of the throne encouraged claimants like Henry Tudor to challenge him for the crown. However, following Henry Tudor's seizure of the throne in 1485 he became the target of claimants who thought of him as the usurper and their claim to be superior. Therefore the first two years of Henry's reign would define his kingship and either strengthen his hold on the throne or weaken it.

Claim to the throne

Henry's claim to the throne was open to challenge because it was so weak. He was well aware that recent history was against him. Richard III's two-year reign had been successfully challenged so Henry knew that he must do all he could to consolidate his hold on the throne.

- Henry's claim came through his mother, Margaret Beaufort, who was a direct descendant of Edward III by the marriage of his third son, John of Gaunt, Duke of Lancaster, to Katherine Swynford. However, the fact that John and Katherine's son John Beaufort (Margaret's grandfather) had been born prior to their marriage weakened any future claim to the throne by this line of descent.
- Henry inherited royal blood from his father, Edmund Tudor. Edmund's French mother, Catherine, had been married to Henry V before she became the wife of Edmund's Welsh father, Owen. Edmund was the half-brother of Henry VI, who raised him to the peerage by creating him Earl of Richmond. Therefore, Henry VII was the half-nephew of the King of England and a member of the extended royal family.
- In reality Henry's claim to the throne rested on his victory in battle. That he had defeated and killed King Richard III was regarded as a sign that God had approved of Henry's assumption of power.

Keeping the throne

Henry VII aimed to maintain his hold on the throne and establish his dynasty by securing the unchallenged succession of his descendants. His policies at home and abroad were shaped and dictated by this aim. Therefore, his goals were simple: to secure his throne and strengthen his dynasty.

Spot the mistake   a

Below is a sample exam question and a paragraph written in answer to this question. Why does this paragraph not get high praise? What is wrong with the focus of the answer in this paragraph?

How far do you agree that Henry VII's claim to the throne was weak?

> Henry's claim to the throne was weak because his father was an earl and not a king. His grandfather was not even an Englishman; he was a Welsh squire. Henry's claim through inheritance was weak because it descended through the female line. Henry was an exiled earl who took a gamble on winning the throne by invading England and facing Richard III in battle.

Support or challenge?   a

Below is a sample exam question which asks to what extent you agree with a specific statement. Below is a list of general statements which are relevant to the question. Using your own knowledge and the information on the opposite page decide whether these statements support or challenge the statement in the question.

How far do you agree that the main reason Henry VII succeeded in establishing the dynasty in the years 1485–99 was the strength of his royal connections?

	SUPPORT	CHALLENGE
Henry VII was descended from Edward III		
Henry VII was a hard-working and energetic monarch		
Henry VII was the half-nephew of Henry VI		
Henry VII had the support of the Pope and the Church		
Henry VII controlled the nobility		
Henry VII married Elizabeth, the daughter of Edward IV		

Securing the Crown

The impact of the battle of Bosworth, 1485

Henry Tudor, Earl of Richmond, was a usurper whose claim to the throne rested on his victory in battle. Having defeated and killed King Richard III, it was considered a sign that God had approved of Henry's seizure of power. However, Henry's victory at **Bosworth** did not guarantee his survival and for the first two years of his reign his hold on the throne remained precarious.

Measures to secure his throne

With little knowledge of England and limited experience in government, Henry knew that he had to prove himself a strong king. In an era of personal monarchy the ruler was responsible for policy, which meant that everything depended on the King's energy, interest and willingness to work.

In order to retain full control of his kingdom Henry would have to
- establish effective government
- maintain law and order
- control the nobility
- secure the Crown's finances.

He would also need sound advice, friends abroad and success in defeating the challenges to his throne.

Henry put in place a series of measures to secure his throne:
- He dated his reign from the day before Bosworth. Therefore, Richard and his supporters could be declared traitors which meant that their estates could be seized.
- He arranged his coronation before the first meeting of parliament and before his marriage to Elizabeth of York. Thus it could never be said that parliament made him King.
- The birth of a son and heir, Arthur, in September 1486 helped establish the dynasty.
- He enlisted the support of the Church and gained control of the nobility.
- He secured the support of the Pope and the Kings of France and Spain, who recognised the legitimacy of his kingship.

The roles of the Yorkist and Lancastrian factions

To maintain his hold on the throne Henry would have to manage the rival **Yorkist** and **Lancastrian** factions both at court and in the country. Following their defeat at Bosworth there were still a number of important Yorkists alive. One of the most dangerous was Edward IV's sister, **Margaret of Burgundy**. To heal the rift between the competing factions Henry married Elizabeth of York, the daughter of King Edward IV. This united the Houses of Lancaster and York and dissuaded many Yorkists from challenging Henry.

Surviving Yorkist nobility were either pardoned or killed.
- **Edward, Earl of Warwick** – The ten-year-old Warwick was sent to the Tower of London. He remained in prison until 1499, when he was executed.
- **John de la Pole**, Earl of Lincoln – Lincoln was invited to join the **King's Council**. He remained loyal until 1487, when he fled the court and was killed at the battle of Stoke.
- **Thomas Howard**, Earl of Surrey, and Henry Percy, Earl of Northumberland – Both were pardoned because they were prepared to work with the new regime.
- Francis, Lord Lovell, and Humphrey and Sir Thomas Stafford – They were executed because they were unwilling to work with Henry.

! Support or challenge?

a

Below is a sample exam question which asks how far you agree with a specific statement. Below this is a series of general statements which are relevant to the question. Using your own knowledge and the information on the opposite page decide whether these statements support or challenge the statement in the question and tick the appropriate box.

How far do you agree that Henry VII's success in securing his hold on the throne was largely due to the support he received from abroad?

	SUPPORT	CHALLENGE
Henry dated his reign from the day before Bosworth		
Henry was victorious at the battle of Bosworth		
The birth of a son and heir established the dynasty		
Henry controlled the nobility		
The Pope and the King of Spain recognised his kingship		
Warwick was executed in 1499		
Henry successfully dealt with the Yorkist factions		
Margaret of Burgundy plotted against Henry VII		

⚡ Eliminate irrelevance

a

Below is a sample exam question and a paragraph written in answer to this question. Read the paragraph and identify parts of the paragraph that are not directly relevant to the question. Draw a line through the information that is irrelevant and justify your deletions in the margin.

How accurate is it to say that Henry VII's prospects of holding on to his throne improved significantly after the birth of a son and heir?

In some respects it is fair to say that Henry VII's prospects of holding on to his throne improved significantly after the birth of Prince Arthur. Henry deliberately chose the name Arthur to impress his subjects because it linked the Tudor dynasty to a glorious past. Securing a son and heir may have convinced his subjects that he was here to stay and that the dynasty was likely to survive. Richard III did not have a son and heir so he was forced to nominate his nephew John de la Pole as his successor. The fact that Arthur was the son of Henry of Richmond and Elizabeth of York did much to unite the Lancastrian and Yorkist factions. Arthur's birth symbolised the union of York and Lancaster and helped end the dynastic conflict that had dominated English politics in the 30 years before Henry VII's accession in 1485.

Challenges to Henry VII's Crown: Lambert Simnel, 1486–87

REVISED

Challenges to Henry VII's Crown

As a usurper himself, Henry was well aware that he was likely to face challenges to his crown. What he had done to Richard III in 1485 others might do to him. The two most serious challengers to his Crown were the Pretenders, **Lambert Simnel** and **Perkin Warbeck**.

The careers of Simnel and Warbeck were of great significance to Henry VII. They presented a dangerous challenge to his hold on the Crown because:
● they gained the support of some powerful English nobles such as the Earl of Lincoln
● they were entangled with other European states, particularly Burgundy and Scotland
● their claims to the throne lasted for a long time – 12 years.

Lambert Simnel, 1486–87

Simnel was the 10-year-old son of an organ maker who was taken as a pupil by an Oxford priest, Richard Symonds. Symonds passed Simnel off as one of the princes in the Tower, Richard of York. However, in the light of rumours about the fate of the Earl of Warwick, he seems to have changed his mind and to have decided that Simnel would now impersonate Warwick. After moving to Ireland, Simnel received the support of the Lord Deputy, the Earl of Kildare. Kildare was one of the most powerful nobles in Ireland and his influence enabled Simnel to be crowned King Edward VI in Dublin. Backed by an Irish army, Simnel landed in England where he was supported by the Yorkist nobleman John de la Pole, Earl of Lincoln.

Diplomatic problems

Simnel's claim to the throne caused various diplomatic problems because he received support from Ireland and Burgundy. Throughout the **Hundred Years' War** against France, Burgundy had been England's main ally. It was also the main outlet for the sale of English cloth. However, Margaret, the Dowager Duchess of Burgundy, sister of Edward IV and Richard III, had supported the Yorkists in the recent civil war and was only too willing to provide 2,000 **mercenaries** for Simnel's cause. Fortunately for Henry, English support for Simnel was very limited, which enabled him to defeat the rebels at the battle of Stoke in 1487.

Henry VII deals with the rebels

As a deterrent to others in the future, those nobles who had fought at Stoke were dealt with swiftly in Henry's second parliament, which met from November to December 1487. Henry **attainted** 28 of them and their lands were confiscated. Henry never again faced an army composed of his own subjects on English soil, although further rebellions did follow. The episode acted as a warning to Henry as it showed how vulnerable his kingship was, that the country was still unsettled and that his hold on the throne was fragile.

! Simple essay style

Below is a sample exam question. Use your own knowledge and the information on the opposite page to produce a plan for this question. Choose four general points, and provide three pieces of specific information to support each general point. Once you have planned your essay, write the introduction and conclusion for the essay. The introduction should list the points to be discussed in the essay. The conclusion should summarise the key points and justify which point was the most important.

How accurate is it to say that in the years 1486–87 Lambert Simnel was never a serious threat to Henry VII's kingship?

! Spectrum of importance

Below is a sample exam question and a list of general points which could be used to answer the question. Use your own knowledge and the information on the opposite page to reach a judgement about the importance of these general points to the question posed.

Write numbers on the spectrum below to indicate their relative importance. Having done this, write a brief justification of your placement, explaining why some of these factors are more important than others. The resulting diagram could form the basis of an essay plan.

How far was Henry VII's success in defeating the challenges to his throne in the years 1485–99 due to his victory at the battle of Stoke (1487)?

1 Warbeck's capture and execution

2 Victory in battle is seen as a sign of God's support

3 The French King abandons Warbeck

4 The death of the Earl of Lincoln at Stoke

5 Simnel is pardoned and employed in the King's service

6 Victory in battle enhances Henry VII's reputation

← Least important   Most important →

Challenges to Henry VII's Crown: Perkin Warbeck, 1491–99

Perkin Warbeck, 1491–99

In the autumn of 1491 Perkin Warbeck, a 17-year-old from Tournai in France, arrived in Ireland on a Breton merchant's ship. He seems to have impressed the townsfolk, who assumed that he might be the Earl of Warwick. Warbeck denied this, claiming instead to be Richard, Duke of York, whose murder in the Tower was assumed but had never been proved.

The conspiracy achieved international recognition from France, Burgundy, the **Holy Roman Empire** and Scotland.

France

Charles VIII (1483–98) welcomed Warbeck at the French court and by the summer of 1492 approximately 100 English Yorkists had joined him in Paris. However, the Treaty of Étaples, which Henry VII negotiated with France in November, meant that he had to leave, so he fled to Flanders where he was accepted by Margaret of Burgundy as her nephew.

Burgundy

It is unlikely that Margaret believed Warbeck to be Richard, Duke of York but, in the absence of any genuine Yorkist claimant at liberty, supporting him would have been her best opportunity to dislodge Henry. She calculated that faithful Yorkists would be prepared to back anyone in order to challenge Henry VII's right to the throne.

Holy Roman Empire

Not content with Margaret's support alone, Warbeck found a more influential patron when Maximilian, the newly elected Holy Roman Emperor, recognised him as Richard IV in 1494. However, Maximilian did not have the resources available to finance an invasion of England.

Scotland

Warbeck's attempt to invade England at Deal in Kent in July 1495 was a fiasco. He failed to gather sufficient local support and set sail for Ireland. Warbeck laid siege to the town of Waterford for 11 days without success and then departed for Scotland, where James IV gave him refuge and support. It is difficult to be certain how far James was convinced by Warbeck, if at all, but he did go so far as to give him his cousin in marriage together with an annual pension of £1,200. He also prepared a force to invade England.

These actions were enough to challenge Henry's crown but fortunately for him, the Scottish invasion of England was a disaster. Warbeck received no support south of the border and retreated.

Warbeck's failure

Warbeck returned to Ireland in July 1497, hoping for more success there. However, he found that even Kildare was temporarily loyal to Henry, so he set sail for the south-west of England hoping, as a last resort, to find support from this traditionally rebellious area. Again he was to be disappointed; having landed in Devon, he was driven out of Exeter and Taunton and only a few thousand people joined him. Within a fortnight it was all over, and Warbeck once again abandoned his followers. This time he fled to the sanctuary of Beaulieu Abbey in Hampshire. In August 1497 he was persuaded to give himself up.

Henry allowed Warbeck to remain at Court with his young Scottish bride, but he escaped in 1498. He was recaptured, publicly humiliated and then imprisoned in the Tower alongside the Earl of Warwick.

Warwick, weary of imprisonment, was persuaded by Warbeck to plan an escape – but they failed. In 1499, Warbeck was charged with trying to escape yet again and this time he was hanged. The Earl of Warwick was found guilty of treason and was executed a week later.

Write the question   **a**

The following source relates to the challenges to Henry VII's Crown by Perkin Warbeck. Having read the pages dealing with Warbeck's challenge to Henry VII's throne, write an exam-style question using the source. Remember, the question must focus on two enquiries.

Assess the value of the source for revealing

_____

and

_____

Explain your answer, using the source, the information given about its origin and your own knowledge about the historical context.

SOURCE 1

From a letter written by the Spanish ambassador to England, Roderigo De Puebla, to King Ferdinand and Queen Isabella of Spain. It was written on 3 July 1495 at the Spanish ambassador's residence in London.

Friday, the 3rd of July 1495, the *so-called* Duke of York came to England with all the ships and troops he had been able to obtain from the Duchess Margaret, the Archduke, and Flanders. A portion of his troops disembarked, but the people rose up in arms against them without the intervention of a single soldier of the King. The peasants of the adjacent villages made great havoc on the troops who had disembarked, and if the vessels had not been at hand not a single man of them would have escaped alive. A hundred and fifty were slain, and eighty made prisoners, among whom were eight captains, two of them being Spaniards, Don Fulano de Guevara (he is said to be a brother or nephew of Don Ladron) and Diego el Coxo (the Lame), the name which all the villagers gave him, saying, that the *King* came, and that he may go to his father and mother, who still live in France, and are well known; and they hold it to be as true as Gospel, as it really is, that this affair is like that of the Duke of Clarence, who was crowned King of Ireland, and afterwards discovered to be the son of a barber. They had no great reasons for congratulating themselves, and had gone, it is believed, to Ireland or Scotland; for it is not probable that they would return to Flanders, because the whole of that country is almost ruined, in consequence of their staying there, the King of England not having permitted any commerce with the Flemings, in which their principal riches and their life consists. Doctor De Puebla is very sorry for these foolish things, for such are they generally believed to be by those who have any knowledge of the affair. Certainly, if the King of the Romans (the Holy Roman Emperor) uphold the Duke of York and his supporters, it would be very difficult to conclude what your Highnesses wish. I think that all that the King of the Romans does is done by the instigation of the King of France. If your Highnesses had taken care earlier of the matter, all this would have been avoided. Nevertheless, it is not too late, even now, if your Highnesses like it.

Challengers from abroad: Treaties and diplomacy

Henry VII and the challengers from abroad

Henry's vulnerable position meant that non-intervention in European politics was essential if he was to stave off challenges to his throne from abroad. Therefore Henry's foreign policy was designed to give him time to consolidate his position. Dynastic threats dominated his dealings with foreign rulers, which explains why the issue of security lay at the heart of his dealings with France, Scotland, Ireland and Burgundy.

Henry's aim in foreign policy was defensive because of the nature of his succession – by usurpation. There were several claimants to his throne who successfully sought aid from foreign powers. Consequently, Henry had to be constantly on his guard against possible invasion.

The most vulnerable border was the northern one with Scotland; as Pope Sixtus V remarked, England was 'only half an island'. Scotland was traditionally the back door into England, and one with which the French were particularly familiar. However, Henry could not afford to ignore Wales, through which his own armed invasion had come, or Ireland, which was volatile and prone to challenging the authority of the English Crown.

However, Henry's most dangerous adversary was Edward IV's sister, Margaret, Duchess of Burgundy. Margaret's support for Henry VII's enemies was persistent and significant. She had the means to fund plots, rebellions and armies and the iron will to support and maintain Henry's opponents over a long period of time.

The power of diplomacy

Henry used diplomacy to develop a network of alliances and trade agreements to help cement his relationship with neighbouring European states. In this way Henry hoped to prevent his enemies from gaining sustained support from abroad. The following treaties and agreements were significant milestones in Henry's European diplomacy.

- Redon, 1489 – Henry promised to defend Brittany's independence from France and support her with troops should the French invade. It failed to prevent France from taking over Brittany in 1491, however.
- Medina del Campo, 1489 – Henry entered into a defensive alliance and trade agreement with Spain, the most powerful country in Europe, which was ratified by the promise of marriage between Henry's son Arthur and Ferdinand and Isabella's daughter, **Catherine of Aragon**. This agreement remained intact until the end of Henry VII's reign.
- Étaples, 1492 – Henry and Charles VIII made peace. The French agreed not to support Warbeck. The two nations maintained an uneasy peace until the end of Henry VII's reign.
- *Magnus Intercursus*, 1496 – Trading relations were resumed between England and Burgundy after the embargo of 1493.
- Truce of Ayton, 1497 – Henry and King James of Scotland agreed to cease hostilities. The Scots promised not to support Warbeck.
- Ayton, 1502 (the Treaty of Perpetual Peace) – The truce became permanent with the signing of this treaty.

! Complete the paragraph a

Below is a sample exam question and a paragraph written in answer to this question.

The paragraph contains a point and specific examples, but lacks a concluding analytical link back to the question. Complete the paragraph adding this link back to the question in the space provided.

How successful was Henry VII's foreign policy in the years 1485–99?

Henry's foreign policy was careful, measured and subordinated to his primary aims of securing and maintaining his kingship of England. He did not have the money to fight wars, which is why he followed a largely non-interventionist foreign policy. Where possible he avoided antagonising his continental neighbours, preferring instead to encourage friendship by concluding treaties and alliances. However, Henry was not prepared to tolerate any foreign power threatening his security by supporting or funding rival claimants, such as the Pretenders Simnel and Warbeck. Overall,

_____

_____

⦿ Spectrum of importance a

Below is a sample exam question and a list of general points which could be used to answer the question. Use your own knowledge and the information on the opposite page to reach a judgement about the importance of these general points to the question posed. Write numbers on the spectrum below to indicate their relative importance. Having done this, write a brief justification of your placement, explaining why some of these factors are more important than others. The resulting diagram could form the basis of an essay plan.

How successful was Henry VII's diplomacy in the years 1485–99?

1 Redon

2 Medina del Campo

3 Étaples

4 *Magnus Intercursus*

5 Truce of Ayton

6 Treaty of Ayton

Least important ←——————————————————————→ Most important

Challengers from abroad: Burgundy, France, Scotland and Ireland

Burgundy (the Netherlands)

Burgundy provided the greatest threat to Henry because Edward IV's sister, Margaret, was married to the ruler, Charles the Bold. Margaret supported the Pretenders Lambert Simnel (1487) and Warbeck (1491–99) with finance and mercenary troops. She also threatened the important English cloth industry because Burgundy was a major trading partner of England. In fact, in 1493 Henry placed a temporary embargo on commercial dealings with the Netherlands because of Philip, Duke of Burgundy, and Margaret's aid for Warbeck. This embargo hurt England's lucrative trade as much as, if not more than, the Netherlands'. Burgundy ceased to be a threat after Margaret's death in 1503.

France

Relations between France and England had been harmonious up to 1488, but this changed when France threatened the independence of Brittany. Henry announced his intention to assert his claim to the French Crown and sent an army across the Channel in 1492, where they laid siege to Boulogne. King Charles VIII wished to avoid war and agreed to sign the Treaty of Étaples in 1492. Charles promised not to give any aid to English rebels, particularly Warbeck. He also agreed to pay most of Henry's campaign costs and to pay an annual pension of £5,000. Thereafter France ceased to be a serious threat to Henry's throne.

Scotland

The most vulnerable part of Henry VII's kingdom was its northern border with Scotland. Scotland was England's traditional enemy, made more dangerous because of the Scots' long-held alliance with France. Relations between Scotland and England were always tense, but Henry was faced by a serious challenge to his throne when King James IV offered Perkin Warbeck his support in 1495. The Scottish-supported challenge to Henry VII's crown lasted two years, until James IV lost faith in Warbeck and decided instead to seek peace with Henry. The Truce of Ayton was concluded in 1497, becoming a full treaty of peace in 1502. The treaty was sealed in 1503 by the marriage of James IV to Henry VII's daughter, Margaret. Thereafter Scotland ceased to be a problem for Henry.

Ireland

In 1487 Simnel received the support of the most powerful noblemen in Ireland, the Earl of Kildare, who arranged the Pretender's coronation in Dublin. After Simnel's defeat at the battle of Stoke in 1487, Kildare was reluctant to support another Pretender – but, after much persuasion, he did so in 1492 when he recognised Warbeck's claim to the throne. In 1494, Henry VII appointed **Sir Edward Poynings**, one of his most trusted advisers, as **Lord Deputy**. Poynings' main task was to pacify the most rebellious areas and to impose a system of government that would ensure Ireland's future obedience to the English Crown. Thereafter Ireland posed no problem for Henry VII.

! Simple essay style

Below is a sample exam question. Use your own knowledge and the information on the opposite page to produce a plan for this question. Choose four general points, and provide three pieces of specific information to support each general point. Once you have planned your essay, write the introduction and conclusion for the essay. The introduction should list the points to be discussed in the essay. The conclusion should summarise the key points and justify which point was the most important.

'Scotland posed a greater threat to Henry VII's rule than Burgundy in the years 1485–1499.' How far do you agree with this statement?

⚡ RAG – Rate the timeline

Below is a sample exam question and a timeline. Read the question, study the timeline and, using three coloured pens, put a Red, Amber or Green star next to the events to show:

- Red: events and policies that have no relevance to the question
- Amber: events and policies that have some significance to the question
- Green: events and policies that are directly relevant to the question

1. How far do you agree that Henry VII's foreign policy made a significant contribution to defeating the foreign challenges to his security?

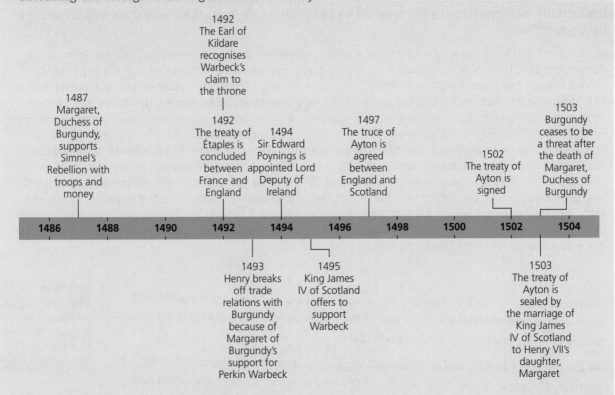

Now repeat the activity with the following question:

2. How far do you agree that the main threat to Henry VII's security in the years 1485–99 came from Margaret of Burgundy?

Exam focus

Below is a source, question and sample answer on the events connected with Henry VII's victory at the battle of Stoke in 1487.

Assess the value of the source for revealing the reasons why Henry VII won the battle of Stoke and why he believed that there would be further challenges to his throne. Explain your answer, using the source, the information given about its origin and your own knowledge about the historical context.

SOURCE 1

From Polydore Vergil's English History, *which he wrote between 1503 and 1513. This extract is focused on the events and people connected with the battle of Stoke in 1487.*

The battle was fought boldly and bitterly on both sides. The Germans, experienced in war, who were in the front line, yielded little to the English in valour; while Martin Schwartz their leader was not inferior to many in his spirit and strength. The Irish, on the other hand, though they fought most spiritedly, were nonetheless slain before the others, being according to their custom devoid of body armour; their slaughter striking no little terror into the other combatants. For some time the contest was even, but at last the royal vanguard, which alone was engaged and sustained the battle, charged the enemy with such impetus that first of all it caused the death of some of the enemy leaders and then put to flight the remainder, who in the course of the fleeing were either captured or killed. It was only then, when the battle was over, that it became all too evident how much boldness there had been in the enemy army; for all their leaders were slain in that place. Lambert the false boy king was captured but was granted his life, since the innocent lad was too young to have given offence.

His enemies defeated, the king was greatly pleased in that he had thus escaped not only the immediate danger, but also the future threat which he feared more. For when he had noticed that his opponents' forces, though much smaller in number and inferior in strength, had come against him with such resolution and had in the end descended into the fray with so little hesitation, he suspected that there must be yet further members of the conspiracy who, at an opportune time and place, would join with them. Therefore, when he saw the enemy line clearly waver in the battle, he ordered that John earl of Lincoln should not be killed so that he might learn from him more concerning the conspiracy. But it is said that the soldiers declined to spare the earl, fearful lest by chance it would happen that the sparing of one man's life would lead to the loss of many. Having gathered the spoils of the slain and committed their bodies for burial, the king proceeded to Lincoln, taking with him a number of captives whom he punished to death. Thence he sent Christopher Urswick with the standard, which he had used against the enemy whom he had defeated, to Walsingham, to give thanks for the victory in the shrine of the Blessed Virgin and to place the standard there as a memorial to the blessing received from God.

This source is useful in revealing some of the reasons why Henry VII feared that the battle of Stoke was the beginning, rather than the end, of the challenges to his throne – but it is more valuable for explaining how and why he won the battle.

The source is very useful in explaining how and why Henry won at Stoke. It states that the 'slaughter' of the Irish struck 'terror into the other combatants', which may have caused them to lose heart. It goes on to say that the key turning point in the battle was the contribution of Henry VII's 'vanguard', which 'charged the enemy with such impetus that first of all it caused the death of some of the enemy leaders and then put to flight the remainder, who in the course of the fleeing were either captured or killed'. This suggests that the vanguard was made up of the King's best equipped and most experienced troops and that their intervention at a crucial moment in a contest that had 'for some time' been 'even' was a game changer. Historians know that the German mercenaries hired by Margaret of Burgundy were probably the best troops on the field of battle, but they were too few in number to make a significant difference. For example, the source states that the Germans were 'fierce', 'in the front line' and that they 'yielded little to the English in valour'. Their commander, Martin Schwartz, is

This is an effective, if brief, introduction that focuses on the question and offers an opinion.

described as a 'leader ... not inferior to many in his spirit and strength'. This suggests that if Margaret had been able to fund a larger force of Germans beyond the 2,000 she paid for, Simnel and his Yorkist backers might have stood a better chance of winning. The source seems to suggest that Henry was relieved to have won the battle – 'His enemies defeated, the King was greatly pleased in that he had thus escaped'. ●

This paragraph offers a good discussion of the content of the extract whilst providing appropriate quoted passages. It also offers an explanation and refers back to the question. Furthermore, it offers some context to the circumstances surrounding the battle.

Although this source is useful for understanding some of the reasons why Henry won the battle, it could be argued that this source does not provide a full picture of what happened at Stoke. For example, at no point does the author of the source suggest that Henry's leadership was responsible for the victory. Historians believe that the victory was due in large part to the weaknesses of the opposition rather than to the superior numbers and generalship of the King or his nobles. Only one part of the King's army – the vanguard – proved worthy of praise. The source praises Schwartz but does not name the military commanders employed by the King, such as the Earl of Oxford, who is credited with winning the battle because of his superior generalship. Moreover, the source states opinion rather than fact, so its value is limited. ●

This paragraph provides some attempt to evaluate within a wider context.

The source hints at why Henry did not overly celebrate the victory in battle – because he thought it simply marked the beginning of a long campaign by his enemies to remove him from the throne. The source states that he was pleased to have 'escaped not only the immediate danger, but also the future threat which he feared more'. The reason for this is because having 'noticed that his opponents' forces, though much smaller in number and inferior in strength, had come against him with such resolution and had in the end descended into the fray with so little hesitation, he suspected that there must be yet further members of the conspiracy'. This is opinion rather than fact because Henry could not know this in 1487. The fact that Henry VII was proved correct that Stoke did not mark the end of the challenges against him suggests that the King knew more than the author of the source about the threats against him. That the King wished to capture Lincoln alive does suggest that he thought he might have some useful information about his enemies.

This paragraph attempts to deal with the second enquiry, though the explanation is not as sure or confident as in the first enquiry. There is weak substantiation of the evaluation.

Historians may agree with this, as the source is based on opinion rather than fact so cannot reveal the full extent of the challenge facing Henry or the lack thereof. The fact that it is an opinion-based source makes it ideal for understanding Henry's views. However, it is from a history sponsored by the King, so it does not reveal the full extent of the challenges facing him and whether he was right to fear that the battle was the beginning rather than the end of the challenges to his throne. ●

This paragraph extends the range of the answer by offering a more rounded conclusion to the two enquiries but it lacks conviction.

This is a good answer. The candidate engages with the question and analyses the source material with varying degrees of effectiveness, though it is clear that the treatment of the two enquiries is somewhat uneven. There is clear evidence of evaluation and it is evident that the candidate is weighing the evidence and attempting to discuss in a reasoned way what can be said on the basis of it. The candidate is clearly aware of the wider context and does attempt, though not always successfully, to integrate this into the answer. On the other hand, there is a lack of development in places and weak substantiation of the evaluation. The candidate does attempt to offer a valid, if limited, conclusion.

Range of explanation

It would be useful to look at this answer through the eyes of the examiner. The examiner will look for a range of explanation. In the margin, write a word or phrase which sums up each specific explanation as it appears. Good answers present at least three explanations and discuss each one in a separate paragraph. Also, highlight or underline where any attempts are made to show links between explanations or where prioritisation occurs.

2 Challenging religious changes, 1533–37

The impact of the Henrician religious changes, 1533–37

The King's Great Matter

The religious changes initiated by Henry VIII and his chief minister, **Thomas Cromwell**, stemmed from the King's desire to **annul** his marriage to Catherine of Aragon. Having failed to provide a son and heir, Henry looked to replace Catherine with his new love interest, **Anne Boleyn**. Henry hoped that Anne would succeed where Catherine had failed. The process of securing the annulment of Henry VIII's marriage is known as the King's Great Matter because it occupied royal and government business for over seven years between 1527 and 1534.

The break with Rome

To secure the annulment of his marriage, Henry needed the Pope's approval – but this was not forthcoming. In an effort to force the Pope into granting the annulment, the King was persuaded by Cromwell to put pressure on the Church. This action set in motion a chain of events that culminated in the unintended break with Rome in 1534. By forcing the Catholic Church in England to support the King's annulment, Cromwell hoped that the Pope would be forced to follow suit. However, this did not happen and as each year passed the pressure exerted by Henry and Cromwell on the Church in England increased. This Reformation in religion was accomplished with the active support of parliament, which was managed with great skill by Cromwell.

The Act of Supremacy, 1534

A combination of political and legal pressure exerted through the so-called **Reformation Parliament** (1529–36) resulted in the submission of the English clergy and the gradual cutting of the Church's ties with Rome. As the King's power over the Church in England increased, the Pope's authority diminished. By 1534 Henry was in a position to assume full control over the Church, which resulted in the passing of the **Act of Supremacy**. Thus Henry VIII became supreme head of the Church in England, which gave him the legal authority to make any changes he wished. With the assistance of the Archbishop of Canterbury, **Thomas Cranmer**, Henry set about initiating doctrinal reform.

The King's religious changes

The break with Rome, allied to the proposed reforms of Church doctrine, proved too much for some of Henry's subjects. It led to conflict between Conservatives and Reformers at Court.
- The Conservatives, led by Bishop **Stephen Gardiner** and Thomas Howard, Duke of Norfolk, resisted religious change, wishing to keep the Church Catholic.
- The Reformers, led by Cranmer and Cromwell, were keen to move the Church in a more Protestant direction.

The conflict at Court mirrored the rising discontent in the country. There were some notable casualties of the King's royal supremacy:
- The executions of Sir **Thomas More** and Bishop **John Fisher** (1535)
- The persecution of the **Franciscans** and **Carthusians**. These were two monastic religious orders and members of the **regular clergy** who remained loyal to the Pope.

In 1535 Cromwell initiated a survey to determine the state of the monasteries. The results of the survey were contained in the *Valor Ecclesiasticus* and led to the passing of the Act for the Dissolution of the Monasteries in 1536. The Act of Ten Articles (1536) and the publication of the Bishops' Book in 1537 moved the Church in a distinctly reformist direction.

! Complete the paragraph a

Below is a sample question and a paragraph written in answer to this question.

The paragraph contains a point and specific examples, but lacks a concluding analytical link back to the question. Complete the paragraph, adding this link back to the question in the space provided.

How far do you agree that Henry's desire to secure the succession was mainly responsible for the Act of Supremacy in 1534?

Henry's desire to secure the succession certainly contributed to the Act of Supremacy but the Pope's refusal to grant the annulment is also a key factor. An annulment was necessary for the King to remarry because Henry needed a male heir to succeed him. The fact that he had fallen in love with Anne Boleyn was a powerful motive for instigating the Royal Supremacy. Cromwell convinced the King that the Church was at fault for blocking the royal will. A corrupt Church needed reform and a reformed Church, with Henry at its head, would be able to grant the annulment. Overall,

_____

_____

⸬ Spectrum of importance a

Below is a sample exam question and a list of general points which could be used to answer the question. Use your own knowledge and the information on the opposite page to reach a judgement about the importance of these general points to the question posed. Write numbers on the spectrum below to indicate their relative importance. Having done this, write a brief justification of your placement, explaining why some of these factors are more important than others. The resulting diagram could form the basis of an essay plan.

To what extent were Henry VIII's religious changes in the 1530s responsible for the rising tide of conflict and discontent in the kingdom?

1 The Act of Supremacy

2 Political conflict at court

3 The dissolution of the monasteries

4 The roles and personalities of Norfolk, Cranmer and Fisher

5 The *Valor Ecclesiasticus*

6 The annulment

←————————————————————————————→

Least important   Most important

The dissolution of the monasteries

Causes of the dissolution

The principal cause of the dissolution of the monasteries was financial. The Crown was in dire need of an additional permanent source of extra income.

The monasteries were thought to be an easy target because they were already in crisis and it was rumoured that the monastic orders preferred **papal primacy** to royal supremacy. Humanists had condemned them as a drain on the nation's wealth and the monastic vocation had declined to such an extent that many houses were staffed by dwindling numbers of inmates. Fewer than 10,000 monks, friars and nuns, inhabiting over 800 monastic institutions, were sustained by perhaps one-fifth of the cultivated land in England and Wales.

Visitation and the compilation of the *Comperta Monastica* and the *Valor Ecclesiasticus*

Cromwell was the King's **vicegerent** responsible for the day-to-day control of the Church. As a **Lutheran** sympathiser, Cromwell had little time for the monastic way of life. In 1535, he sent his agents to visit every monastery in the kingdom with the aim of compiling a thorough record of their condition and wealth. The visitations resulted in the compilation of the **Comperta Monastica**, recording the condition and conduct of the inmates, and the Valor Ecclesiasticus, recording the net worth and annual income of each monastery.

According to the *Valor*, the net annual income of the Church was put at around £380,000 (£122 million today) whilst the *Comperta* selectively listed the bad behaviour of some monks and nuns. Between them, the *Valor* and the *Comperta* provided a significant amount of ammunition for those determined to justify the closure of the monasteries.

The Act for the Dissolution of the Smaller Monasteries, 1536

The visitations of 1535 and the commissions to compile the *Valor* and *Comperta* led to rumours that the government intended to dissolve the monasteries and to seize their wealth. These fears were born out in part by an Act which was passed by parliament in March 1536. The Act stipulated that all religious houses with an annual income of less than £200 (as assessed in the *Valor Ecclesiasticus*) should be dissolved and that their property should pass to the Crown. It provided for the heads of the houses to be granted a pension and for other members to be offered the option of transferring to a larger house or ceasing to be 'religious' by going out into the world to start a new life. Over 300 houses fell within the category specified by the Act and most of them were dissolved.

The destruction of the remaining monasteries, 1538–40

The Crown continued to close monasteries piecemeal during 1536–37, though this stopped temporarily when the rebellion known as the **Pilgrimage of Grace** broke out (see page 24). When this rebellion had been crushed the dissolution began again. By the time the Act for the Dissolution of the Greater Monasteries was passed in 1539, few monastic institutions remained. By early 1540 all had been closed.

! Mind map

Use the information on the page opposite to add detail to the mind map below to show the causes of the dissolution of the monasteries.

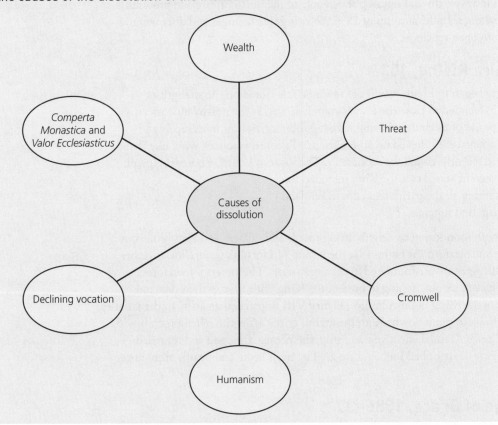

♦ Develop the detail   **a**

Below is a sample exam question and a paragraph written in answer to this question. The paragraph contains a limited amount of detail. Annotate the paragraph to add additional detail to the answer.

> To what extent did the *Valor Ecclesiasticus* contribute to the dissolution of the monasteries between 1536 and 1540?

When Henry VIII assumed the title of Supreme Head of the Church, the monasteries were doomed. The King's title and his supremacy were engineered by Thomas Cromwell, a Lutheran sympathiser and enemy of the monastic vocation. He was determined to impress the King by finding evidence of wrongdoing which would enable him to destroy the monasteries and thereby exploit their wealth. The *Valor Ecclesiasticus* provided Cromwell with the material he needed to convince the King that the dissolution was not only the right thing to do, it was necessary.

The Lincolnshire Rising and the Pilgrimage of Grace

The monasteries offered little opposition to their dissolution because Henry had the law on his side. In 1535 the monks and nuns had sworn an oath to accept Henry's authority as Supreme Head of the Church. However, this did not stop the people of the north of England protesting in defence of the monasteries. In the autumn of 1536 the rising tide of anger and discontent in Lincolnshire turned into open rebellion.

The Lincolnshire Rising, 1536

The Lincolnshire rising began in Louth, when the townspeople rioted on the strength of rumours that the King intended to close the town's church as well as the nearby monastery. The community was proud of its church, having invested substantial sums in its repair and enlargement. The rumours were believed because Cromwell's commissioners, who, like their master, were hated, had recently visited the monastery. The vicar of Louth, Thomas Kendall, made matters worse when he stated that the King intended to:

- confiscate the treasures of all the parish churches in England
- tax baptisms, marriage and funerals.

News of the riot in Louth soon spread to neighbouring towns and villages and riots broke out in Caistor, Horncastle and Sleaford. At Horncastle the bishop of Lincoln's chancellor, together with one of Cromwell's agents, were murdered by an angry mob. The rioters joined forces and marched on the city of Lincoln, hoping to present the King with a list of their demands. Alarmed by the news of the rising in Lincolnshire, Henry VIII dispatched an army under Charles Brandon, Duke of Suffolk, to put it down. With the arrival of the army the rebellion collapsed, as the gentry sued for peace. Denied effective leadership, the people dispersed and returned home. An angry Henry VIII described Lincolnshire as 'The most brute and beastly shire of the whole realm'.

The Pilgrimage of Grace, 1536–37

As the Lincolnshire rising collapsed, the people of Yorkshire rose in rebellion. Fuelled by rumours of wholesale monastic closures and encouraged by news of the Lincolnshire rising, a lawyer, **Robert Aske**, assumed control of the revolt in the East Riding of Yorkshire (see page 26). Adopting the title the Pilgrimage of Grace, Aske revised the Lincolnshire rebels' demands and placed more emphasis on preserving the church and defending the monasteries. As the rebels moved north they recruited additional followers, including members of the gentry – Sir William Babthorpe and Sir Thomas Percy – and nobility – Lord Hussey and Lord Darcy. Soon the rebels numbered more than 30,000.

Preoccupied with regaining control of Lincolnshire, the King did not initially appreciate the seriousness of the Pilgrimage of Grace, and a royal army under the command of Thomas Howard, third duke of Norfolk, took a month to arrive. Outnumbered and playing for time, Norfolk arranged a truce and allowed the rebels to submit a list of their complaints. Aske convened a meeting to draw up the **Pontefract Articles** which were submitted to the King. Henry issued a general pardon while he considered the articles, but before he could come to a decision a new rising broke out, led by **Sir Francis Bigod** (see page 26). Bigod's revolt was put down, but it resulted in Aske's arrest and trial for treason.

Mind map

Use the information on the opposite page to create your own mind map to show the causes of the Pilgrimage of Grace.

Identify an argument

a

Below is a series of definitions, a sample exam question and two sample conclusions. One of the conclusions achieves a high mark because it contains an argument. The other achieves a lower mark because it is contains only description and assertion. Identify which is which. The mark scheme on pages 111–12 will help you.

- **Description:** a detailed account.
- **Assertion:** a statement of fact or an opinion which is not supported by a reason.
- **Reason:** a statement which explains or justifies something.
- **Argument:** an assertion justified with a reason.

To what extent were rumours of a tax on baptisms, marriage and funerals responsible for the outbreak of rebellion in northern England in 1536?

Conclusion 1

Overall, there is clearly some evidence that rumours of a tax on baptisms, marriage and funerals were mainly responsible for the outbreak of rebellion in the north of England in 1536. First, there was the work of Cromwell's commissioners, who went around the northern counties surveying the wealth of the Church. They were distrusted and disliked by the people. Cromwell, too, was hated and blamed for persuading the King to consider imposing these taxes. Northerners tended to resent southerners interfering in their affairs, so they believed the rumours. The rumours that the monasteries were going to be closed were not as important to the people because the proposed taxation on baptisms, marriage and funerals affected them directly.

Conclusion 2

In conclusion, although there is no doubt that rumours of a tax on baptisms, marriage and funerals did contribute to the outbreak of rebellion in the north in 1536 it was only one of a number of causes of the revolt. The key feature here is the word 'rumour', because in a world without the technology to broadcast news, information was transmitted by word of mouth or by written and oral proclamation. This is why the Tudors passed laws against people spreading unfounded rumours. People were determined to defend their Church and their religious way of life, so a tax on such fundamental activities as baptism, marriage and funerals made the population angry as they could not be avoided. To suggest that rumours of a tax on baptisms, marriage and funerals were mainly responsible for the outbreak of rebellion is perhaps going too far. There were other equally significant causes of rebellion such as the closure of the monasteries — another action stimulated by rumour — and the more tangible, and visible, work of Cromwell's commissioners in visiting parish churches and local monasteries.

Leaders in challenge: Robert Aske and Sir Francis Bigod

Robert Aske (1500–37)

Robert was the son of Sir Robert Aske of Aughton, near Selby in Yorkshire. He was a London lawyer with powerful family connections, being a cousin of Henry Clifford, Earl of Cumberland.

Aske never intended to join – let alone lead – a rebellion. He stumbled into the Lincolnshire Rebellion while travelling through the county to London for the beginning of the law term.

Aske was captured and persuaded to join a band of rebels at Sawcliff. Soon Aske was taking the lead in decision-making and organising the rebel bands in the north of the county. Having made contact with the main rebel group at Louth, Aske then travelled to Yorkshire to raise support for the rising there. Recruiting 10,000 men, Aske then entered the city of York where he issued a proclamation that laid out the aims of the rebellion – to preserve and defend the Church.

The Pontefract Articles

Following the collapse of the Lincolnshire revolt, Aske drew up his own list of grievances, wrote his own oath and gave the movement the title of the Pilgrimage of Grace. Aske advanced from York to Pontefract Castle, which he took after a short siege. Among those captured in the castle were its constable, Thomas Lord Darcy, Edward Lee, Archbishop of York, and a number of Yorkshire gentry. Darcy and some of the gentry were persuaded to join the rebellion and they helped Aske draw up the Pontefract Articles, which called for:

- the legitimisation of Princess Mary (the eldest daughter of Henry VIII and the future Queen Mary I)
- Cromwell and others among the King's 'evil councillors' to be dismissed
- a meeting of parliament in York
- an end to the closure of the monasteries
- the restoration of links with the Pope.

The end of the rebellion

A royal army of some 4,000 men under Thomas Howard, Duke of Norfolk was sent by the King to deal with the rebels. However, Norfolk faced a rebel force of over 30,000, so he played for time. The Pontefract Articles were presented to Norfolk, who agreed to issue a pardon and the promise of a parliament to be held at York. Aske accepted the King's invitation to go to Court over Christmas 1536 – but while Aske negotiated an agreement, a renegade member of the gentry, Sir Francis Bigod, led a new rising in January 1537. Aske was blamed for the renewal of rebellion in Yorkshire and was arrested, tried and hanged at York in July 1537.

Sir Francis Bigod (1507–37)

Sir Francis Bigod was the son of Sir John Bigod of Hinderwell, Yorkshire. He was an unlikely rebel because he was a Protestant and had been one of Cromwell's agents in the north. He was a **Justice of the Peace** and a member of the Reformation Parliament. Bigod even helped compile the *Valor Ecclesiasticus* and enforced the Royal Supremacy. However, unlike Cromwell, Bigod wanted monasteries reformed rather than dissolved. Bigod initially opposed the Pilgrimage of Grace but after his capture by the rebels he was persuaded to join their cause.

Distrustful of the King and doubtful that Aske would succeed in gaining royal acceptance of the Pontefract Articles, Bigod revived the rebellion in Yorkshire. Bigod's men were defeated and he fled to Cumberland, where he was captured. He was tried and hanged in June 1537.

Delete as applicable

Below is a sample exam question and a paragraph written in answer to this question. Read the paragraph and decide which of the possible options (in bold) is most appropriate. Delete the least appropriate options and complete the paragraph by justifying your selection.

'The rebellions in the north of England posed a very real threat to Henry VIII.' How far do you agree with this statement?

The threat posed by rebellions in the north was **very serious/moderately serious/not serious**. For example, rebel numbers exceeded 30,000 but not all of these were able-bodied men, some were women, and a large number of the men had no military experience. Nevertheless, the size of the rising would have sent shock waves through the royal court because it highlighted the scale of the discontent. This forced the King to send an army against the rebels. In this way, it can be seen that the King and his ministers did feel **seriously threatened/moderately threatened/not threatened** because

_____

_____

Turning assertion into argument

Below is a sample exam question and a series of assertions. Read the exam question and then add a justification to each of the assertions to turn it into an argument.

How significant was the challenge posed by the Pilgrimage of Grace to the government of Henry VIII in the years 1536–37?

The Pilgrimage of Grace posed a significant challenge because

_____

_____

The Pilgrimage of Grace did not pose a significant challenge because

_____

_____

The example set by the rebels in the Pilgrimage of Grace was serious because

_____

_____

The Pilgrimage of Grace can be seen as merely a protest movement which supported rather than opposed Henry VIII and his government

_____

_____

Leaders in suppression: Henry VIII, Thomas Cromwell and the Duke of Norfolk

Henry VIII

Henry's greatest fear was the outbreak of rebellion. He was well aware that the religious changes he introduced were such that some people might be pushed into armed opposition to the Crown and its ministers. In the end, the long-feared rebellion broke out in northern England in late 1536. Beginning in Lincolnshire the rebellion quickly escalated and spread to Yorkshire, acquiring the name 'Pilgrimage of Grace' along the way.

The Pilgrimage of Grace was the largest and, potentially, the most serious rebellion of the sixteenth century. The rebellion grew in strength, attracting between 30,000 and 40,000 people as it broadened geographically to include half a dozen counties in the north.

Dealing with the rebels

Henry's initial reaction was to suppress the rebellion by the use of military force. He ordered the Dukes of Suffolk and Norfolk to deal with the insurgents but their forces, numbering no more than 4,000 men each, were vastly outnumbered by the rebels.

Henry turned to diplomacy and managed to persuade the rebel leader, Robert Aske, of his good intentions. Negotiating through Norfolk, who posed as a sympathiser, Henry conceded to their demands – monastic lands to be restored, Cromwell to be removed and a parliament called to address their wider concerns. Henry also promised a free pardon for all rebels who agreed to disperse and return to their homes.

Duped by a deliberately deceitful King, the rebels dispersed – but in the weeks following the end of the rebellion many, including Aske, were hunted down, arrested, tried and executed.

Thomas Cromwell

There is no doubt that Cromwell played a pivotal role in the Henrician Reformation. As the King's vicegerent in religious affairs, he exerted the most significant influence of any individual (with the possible exception of Thomas Cranmer) on the life of the Church.

Cromwell had a powerful influence in royal circles. He was described by his enemy, Cardinal Reginald Pole, as 'an agent of Satan sent by the devil to lure King Henry to damnation'. This is why the rebels were so determined to get rid of him.

Cromwell responded by cynically using the rebels' loyalty to the King to outmanoeuvre them. He advised Henry to:
- prolong negotiations so as to gain time to raise a larger army
- feign sympathy with the rebels' demands so that a trusting Aske would order his forces to disperse.

Duke of Norfolk

Thomas Howard, Duke of Norfolk, was one of the most powerful and influential figures at Court. Norfolk came to prominence by leading the faction opposed to Henry's chief minister, Cardinal **Thomas Wolsey**. A conservative in religion, Norfolk became a leading critic of the reformers Thomas Cromwell and Thomas Cranmer. However, he was careful not to oppose the King's religious changes.

Although Cromwell's growing power weakened his position at Court, Norfolk never lost the King's trust. It was to Norfolk that the King turned to suppress the Pilgrimage of Grace. Unable to crush the rebellion by military means, Norfolk engineered the defeat of the rebels by deceiving their leader, Aske, and detaching him from his followers by promising to take their demands seriously.

! Simple essay style

Below is a sample exam question. Use your own knowledge and the information on the opposite page to produce a plan for this question. Choose four general points and provide three pieces of specific information to support each general point. Once you have planned your essay, write the introduction and conclusion for the essay. The introduction should list the points to be discussed in the essay. The conclusion should summarise the key points and justify which point was the most important.

'The suppression of the Pilgrimage of Grace in 1537 was due to the efforts of the Duke of Norfolk.' How far do you agree with this statement?

⦾ Support your judgement   **a**

Below is a sample exam question and two basic judgements. Read the exam question and the two judgements. Support the judgement that you agree with more strongly by adding a reason that justifies the judgement.

To what extent was Henry VIII responsible for the suppression of the rebellions in the north in the years 1536–37?

Overall, Henry did more than most to suppress the rebellions because the final decision rested with him

_____

_____

Generally, Henry VIII's success in suppressing the rebellious north owed as much to Cromwell and Norfolk as to his own efforts

_____

_____

Tip: Whichever option you choose you will have to weigh up both sides of the argument. You could use phrases such as 'whereas' or words like 'although' in order to help the process of evaluation.

Failure and impact of the rebellion

Reasons for failure

The Pilgrimage of Grace failed largely because of the naivety of the rebels and their loyalty to Henry VIII. They had been educated by the Church to accept the notion of the **Great Chain of Being**, in which every person's place in society had been ordained by God. They were naive enough to:

- proclaim their loyalty to Henry VIII, wishing only to remove his 'evil councillors'
- trust the King's promises that their complaints would be taken seriously and that they would be pardoned.

In the autumn of 1536 Aske was able to draw upon widespread popular opposition to the direction of Henry's religious policies. Aske had no hesitation in offering the people leadership and organisation, referring to them on one occasion as 'my people'. He made a serious error in agreeing to disband the pilgrimage in return for the promise of a pardon and a parliament. It may be argued that it was the failure of the pilgrims to press home their advantage which allowed Henry to suppress the rebellion. Aske and his co-conspirators achieved none of their aims:

- No parliament in the north of England was ever convened.
- Their grievances were never fully addressed.
- The religious changes continued and accelerated.
- The dissolution of the monasteries continued.
- Cromwell was not dismissed.

Impact

Although the rebellion never seriously threatened the King, it did threaten the maintenance of law and order in the north of England – which is why it was doomed to failure. No King could allow a rebellion to go unpunished, no matter how loyal the rebels claimed to be. It would have set a dangerous precedent. In fact, under interrogation Aske admitted that he had been willing to fight if Henry had not conceded the grievances expressed in the pilgrims' petition.

By deceiving Aske, and by appearing to sympathise with some of their grievances, Henry effectively disarmed and dispersed the rebels. To deter other would-be rebels Henry dealt ruthlessly with the ringleaders – Aske, Bigod and their senior captains. Norfolk was tasked with displaying the Crown's power in the north by deploying military forces in strategic areas and by invoking **martial law**.

Extent of repression

Besides the ringleaders, some two hundred rebels were put to death in the aftermath of the uprisings. Norfolk moved through the northern counties with an armed force, hunting down insurgents. As a result of his efforts:

- 34 insurgents were executed in Lincolnshire.
- 74 rebels perished under martial law in Cumberland and Westmorland.
- The majority of the remainder were hanged in Yorkshire, though some of those who perished came from Lancashire, Durham and Northumberland.

The ringleaders were put on trial and executed:

- Sir Francis Bigod, Sir Thomas Percy, Sir John Bulmer, Sir Stephen Hamerton, Nicholas Tempest, George Lumley, John Pickering, William Wood and Adam Sedbergh were all executed at Tyburn.
- Abbot James Cockerell of Guisborough and Abbot William Thirsk of Fountains were hanged.
- Bulmer's wife, Margaret Cheyne, was shown no mercy for her support for the pilgrims and was burnt at Smithfield.
- Thomas, Lord Darcy, was beheaded on Tower Hill, Sir Robert Constable was hanged at Hull, and Lord Hussey was beheaded at Lincoln. Robert Aske was hanged at York.

Quick quizzes at **www.hoddereducation.co.uk/myrevisionnotes**

ⓘ Establish criteria ⓐ

Below is a sample exam question which requires you to make a judgement. The key term in the question has been underlined. Defining the meaning of the key term can help you establish criteria that you can use to make a judgement.

Read the question, define the key term and then set out two or three criteria based on the key term, which you can use to reach and justify a judgement.

> How accurate is it to say that the Pilgrimage of Grace, 1536–37, failed largely because of the <u>mistakes made by the rebels</u>?

Definition

_____

_____

Criteria to judge the extent to which the Pilgrimage of Grace failed largely because of the naivety of the rebels:

_____

_____

_____

_____

ⓘ Reach a judgement ⓐ

Having defined the key term and established a series of criteria, you should now make a judgement. Consider how far the Pilgrimage of Grace failed largely because of the naivety of the rebels according to each criterion. Summarise your judgements below:

● Criterion 1:

_____

● Criterion 2:

_____

● Criterion 3:

_____

● Criterion 4:

_____

Finally, sum up your judgement. Based on the criteria, how accurate is it to say that the Pilgrimage of Grace failed largely because of the naivety of the rebels?

_____

_____

_____

Tip: Remember you should weigh up evidence of naivety against evidence of failure in your conclusion.

Exam focus

Below is a sample answer on the events connected with the Pilgrimage of Grace. Read the answer to the exam-style question and the comments around it.

How far do you agree that the Pilgrimage of Grace was a spontaneous religious uprising?

The Pilgrimage of Grace was the largest and potentially most serious of the rebellions of the Tudor period. Any rebellion was considered a threat to the Crown and the government of the kingdom because it heightened the risk of political instability and administrative breakdown. Protest and rebellion were also considered to be against the teachings of God because the protestors or rebels were challenging the notion of the Great Chain of Being. It has been suggested by some historians that the Pilgrimage of Grace was planned from the beginning, but others believe that it was spontaneous – a popular uprising by angry people.

This is a general introduction that provides a background rather than exploring the conflicting interpretations of whether the Pilgrimage of Grace was spontaneous or planned.

The rebellions that broke out in northern England, firstly in Lincolnshire and then in Yorkshire, were triggered by immediate grievances rather than any long-standing ones. The people of the north were reacting to the radical religious and economic policies being forced upon them by the King's ministers in London. They were unhappy with the teams of Cromwell's commissioners who were asking too many questions and compiling lists of goods and clerical behaviour. They were also worried about the rumours of high taxes being imposed on sheep and land sales, together with hikes in the price of funerals, marriage and baptisms. These wild rumours were believed by the people of Louth, who left their homes to defend their church from Cromwell's hated commissioners. They feared the church would be ransacked and perhaps even torn down. With the support of the clergy in Lincolnshire, the people were stirred up into joining together to resist Cromwell's commissioners. Soon 10,000 people had joined together and a local landowner, Lord Hussey, assumed command.

This paragraph provides a historical summary of the causes of the rebellion.

The Lincolnshire rising was certainly spontaneous and it ended as quickly as it had started – in a little over a week. When commanded by the King to disperse and go home, the people complied. However, a much larger gathering of people was happening over the border in Yorkshire, where some 20,000 people joined Robert Aske in a protest march on York. They, too, had heard the rumours of Cromwell's plans for taxes, religious reforms and the closure of the monasteries. But they were also inspired by news of the rising in Louth. Aske convinced his followers that Cromwell was to blame and that the King did not know what was going on. He was joined by two powerful landowners, Lord Darcy and Lord Hussey. The rebels even took Pontefract Castle, which frightened the King. This, too, was a spontaneous uprising which only acquired structure and a coherent plan after the people had risen up in anger. Aske called his followers 'pilgrims in search of God's truth', which suggests that they were not rebels.

This paragraph is the first to deal specifically with the interpretation offered in the opening quotation – that the Pilgrimage of Grace was a spontaneous religious uprising. If this is taken in conjunction with the previous paragraph then a case is being made.

However, some historians believe that the Pilgrimage of Grace was not spontaneous but was part of a bigger plan involving intrigue at Court. For example, G.R. Elton believes that the rebellion was planned from the beginning and that it had some 'spontaneous moments'. He believed it was a political rising organised by members of the Aragonese faction at Court. They had been displaced by Cromwell following the death of their patron, Catherine of Aragon. For example, Hussey and Darcy had first contemplated a rebellion as early as 1534. The Pontefract Articles drawn up by Aske and his fellow conspirators reveal a number of political demands alongside the religious, economic and social grievances. This would suggest a planned rebellion. Darcy's all-too-easy surrender of Pontefract Castle suggests that he was working to a planned timetable.

This paragraph provides the counter-argument based mainly on one historian's opinion – G.R. Elton. It explores political causes and factions at court to support a planned rebellion.

There is an alternative explanation. It is possible that the peasants' rising was spontaneous because of their anger and what they saw as Cromwell's attempt to ruin their churches and monasteries. But the involvement of the gentry was not spontaneous because once the rebellion had begun, the landowners became involved deliberately, either through fear of resisting the angry commons or through manipulation of the people to their own ends.

Although there is some evidence to suggest that the Pilgrimage of Grace was a 'spontaneous religious uprising', there is a great deal of uncertainty. This was scarcely an armed uprising seeking military confrontation – and there was never any threat to Henry VIII. They presented themselves as pilgrims who simply wished to preserve their monasteries and defend their churches. They had to blame someone – and who better than Cromwell? Therefore, it is possible to say that the Pilgrimage of Grace may have been spontaneous.

This paragraph extends the range of the essay by introducing an alternative interpretation – both spontaneous and planned, but at different social levels. This is a reasonable suggestion and does suggest that the candidate acknowledges the complexity of the issue.

This is a reasonably good essay. The range of issues identified and supported in this answer demonstrates a reasonable level of appropriate knowledge. The premise of the question is addressed throughout, with some attempt to evaluate by exploring the counter-argument. There is a limited attempt to reach a judgement and more could have been done to develop the counter-argument that the rebellion was not spontaneous but planned. Also, the candidate does not fully explore the religious aspect mentioned in the quotation. No reference is made to the rebels outside Yorkshire, such as in Durham and Northumberland, and too little is said about the impact of the Lincolnshire rising. Lapses in style should not be penalised too heavily; nor should lapses into narrative/description.

The conclusion is rather confused and is not sure which side to support. It could have been clearer and could have extended the debate, with additional examples to flesh out one interpretation against the other.

Maintaining focus

This essay is successful because it maintains a strong focus on the question throughout. There is a lot of detail on the Pilgrimage of Grace but other paragraphs are also related to the Pilgrimage of Grace where possible. Go through the essay and underline every mention of the phrase 'Pilgrimage of Grace'. Next, look at an essay you have written and underline your use of key words. Can you improve on your own efforts in the light of what you have seen here?

2 Challenging religious changes, 1533–37

3 Agrarian discontent: Kett's Rebellion, 1549

The social and economic reasons for rebellion

Social and economic problems

The first part of the reign of Edward VI was dominated by the personality and power of **Edward Seymour**, Duke of Somerset, who, as **Lord Protector**, ruled the kingdom on behalf of the boy king.

Socially and economically, the period involved considerable change marked by price inflation, growing population, rising unemployment, **enclosures** and the **debasement of the coinage**. Added to the changes in religion, all of this generated a sense of national crisis.

The reasons for rebellion

The steadily rising population was accompanied by a rise in inflation, which meant that the living standards of the masses declined. Work was more difficult to find, which led to migration from the countryside into the towns. This was made worse by the growing instability of the Antwerp cloth market, which led to widespread unemployment among textile workers in East Anglia.

Given that cloth was England's biggest industry, this depression in the cloth trade had serious repercussions for dependent communities across the country. Grain prices, too, rose rapidly – a situation worsened by below-average harvests. By 1549 the country was simmering with discontent.

Somerset was advised to end the debasement of the coinage as a remedy for price inflation, but he refused. Instead, he turned his attention to illegal enclosure – in June 1548 a royal proclamation announced the appointment of commissions to collect evidence and enforce laws restricting enclosures. Somerset's aims were to:
- reduce depopulation and rural poverty
- increase grain production by discouraging sheep grazing.

The Vagrancy Act

The 1547 Vagrancy Act and the sheep tax of 1548 contributed to the growing unrest. The maintenance of public order was very much in the mind of Somerset's administration when it passed the Vagrancy Act of 1547. The harshness of this legislation showed little concern for the poor. The Act was a savage attack on vagrants looking for work, who were seen by the government as a cause of riots and sedition.

Under the new law, any able-bodied person out of work for more than three days was to be branded with a V and sold into slavery for two years. Further offences were to be punished with permanent slavery. The children of vagrants could be taken from their parents and set to work as apprentices in useful occupations. The new law was widely unpopular, and many of the county and urban authorities refused to enforce it. Although it also proposed housing and collections for the disabled, this measure damaged Somerset's reputation for humanitarianism.

The maintenance of law and order

It appears that the government was more concerned with avoiding riot and rebellion than with helping the poor and solving economic problems. This is supported by three proclamations issued in 1548, aimed specifically at maintaining law and order. These proclamations seem like emergency measures passed by a government which realised that the economic and social conditions were getting out of hand and which feared the consequences. Unfortunately for Somerset, he did not fully appreciate the scale of the economic and social crisis facing him, which is why he was surprised by the outbreak of rebellion in 1549. Somerset's failure to deal decisively with the problems facing the government led to his downfall.

Spectrum of importance **a**

Below is a sample question and a list of general points which could be used to answer the question. Use your own knowledge and the information on the opposite page to reach a judgement about the importance of these general points to the question posed. Write numbers on the spectrum below to indicate their relative importance. Having done this, write a brief justification of your placement, explaining why some of these factors are more important than others. The resulting diagram could form the basis of an essay plan.

To what extent was enclosure responsible for the outbreak of rebellion in 1549?

1 Policy and impact of the enclosing of land

2 Somerset's weakness as a ruler

3 Social turmoil and economic difficulties

4 Decline and depression in the cloth trade

5 The Vagrancy Act

6 Breakdown in the notion and principles of the Great Chain of Being

←————————————————————————————→

Least important   Most important

Identify the concept **a**

Below are five sample exam questions based on some of the following concepts:

- **Cause** – questions concern the reasons for something, or why something happened.
- **Consequence** – questions concern the impact of an event, an action or a policy.
- **Change/continuity** – questions ask you to investigate the extent to which things changed or stayed the same.
- **Similarity/difference** – questions ask you to investigate the extent to which two events, actions or policies were similar.
- **Significance** – questions concern the importance of an event, an action or a policy.

Read each of the questions and work out which of the concepts they are based on.

'Opposition to enclosures had little impact on Somerset's rule in the years 1547–49.' How far do you agree with this statement?

How far did the depression in the cloth trade contribute to the outbreak of rebellion in 1549?

How accurate is it to say that Somerset's policies were primarily responsible for the social and economic instability that led to rebellion in 1549?

How accurate is it to say that Somerset's fall from power was the most important consequence of the 1549 rebellions?

'Protector Somerset's power was fundamentally weakened by the 1549 rebellions.' How far do you agree with this statement?

Enclosures and the Duke of Somerset's commission

Enclosures

As a result of rising prices and local food shortages, the level of popular discontent increased. The Privy Council was forced to take measures to appease public agitation but it did not fully appreciate the cause of this discontent. The government blamed all the economic problems on enclosure. It was felt that the fencing-off of common land for sheep pasture and the consequent eviction of husbandmen and cottagers from their homes was the major cause of inflation and unemployment. Proclamations were issued against enclosures, and commissioners were sent out to investigate abuses. This action earned Somerset the title 'the Good Duke'.

Somerset's enclosure commission

In June 1548 Somerset appointed John Hales to lead a six-member commission to investigate enclosure practices in the midland counties. Hales was MP for Preston in Lancashire and during his time in parliament he became an outspoken critic of government policy – particularly its treatment of the poor. Hales' demand for social and economic reform brought him to the attention of Protector Somerset.

The commissioners set about their task with determination but they were often blocked from conducting their surveys by self-interested gentry landowners. This sometimes led to ugly confrontations – as in Buckinghamshire, when people rioted in support of the commissioners, who were being harassed by a local landowner who stood to lose his enclosed fields. Hales was blamed for inciting riots but he strongly denied the charge. One of Hales' opponents was the Earl of Warwick, who demanded his removal from the commission – but Somerset refused.

Impact of the enclosure commission

The enclosure commission proved controversial and divisive. Landlords opposed the commissioners and the common people became frustrated when they failed to resolve enclosure disputes. To the landlords, enclosures were vital if they were to maximise their profits from their estates. The move from arable to pastoral farming – mainly based on sheep and wool – enriched the landlords but led to unemployment among the farm labourers.

As a result, the enclosure commission led to an increase in unrest. Somerset's intervention only made things worse. In trying to support the commissioners, he passed further measures, such as limiting the size of leaseholds and placing a tax on wool. However, whereas many of the landowners were able to evade the wool tax, the poorest in society could not.

This increased the tension between landlords and their tenants. Anger and frustration led to the outbreak of riots in more than a dozen English counties, which escalated into two serious rebellions in Cornwall (mainly concerned with Somerset's religious reforms) and East Anglia. The East Anglian rising, led by **Robert Kett**, proved to be the most serious challenge to the government.

Identify key terms a

Below is a sample exam question which includes a key word or term. Key terms are important because their meaning can be helpful in structuring your answer, developing an argument, and establishing criteria that will help form the basis of a judgement.

> How accurate is it to say that Somerset's enclosure commissions led to the outbreak of riots and rebellion?

- First, identify the key word or term. This will be a word or phrase that is important to the meaning of the question. Underline the word or phrase.
- Second, define the key phrase. Your definition should set out the key features of the phrase or word that you are defining.
- Third, make an essay plan that reflects your definition.
- Finally, write a sentence answering the question that refers back to the definition.

Now repeat the task, and consider how the change in key terms affects the structure, argument and final judgement of your essay.

> How accurate is it to say that Somerset's policy on enclosures proved controversial and divisive by 1549?

Develop the detail a

Below is a sample exam question and a paragraph written in answer to this question. The paragraph contains a limited amount of detail. Annotate the paragraph to add additional detail to the answer.

> How successful was Somerset's enclosure policy in solving the problems associated with high inflation and rising unemployment by 1549?

Between 1547 and 1549 Somerset's government did not succeed in solving the problems associated with high inflation and rising unemployment. Somerset's policies were aimed at promoting arable farming, as opposed to the less labour-intensive pastoral farming. He hoped this would reduce unemployment and bring down inflation. However, he had failed to fully appreciate the scale of the kingdom's social and economic problems, which is why his policy on enclosure was unlikely to work. Overall, it is clear that Somerset did not understand the problems and nor did he have a credible plan to solve them.

The challenge posed by Kett's Rebellion

Kett's Rebellion

East Anglia was the most densely populated and highly industrialised part of the country. Norwich was the second-largest town after London, and was a major textile centre. The causes of the rebellion are symptomatic of the confused nature of discontent in the lower orders against the economic changes. The rising was triggered by unrest over enclosures, high rents and unsympathetic local landlords like Sir John Flowerdew, a lawyer who had bought up Church property in the area.

Flowerdew was also in dispute with a local **yeoman**, Robert Kett, over land. Kett was a tanner and small landowner who had also enclosed common land. Flowerdew tried to turn the rioters against him but Kett retaliated by offering to act as spokesman for them. Kett was to prove an inspirational leader and as such posed a serious threat to the authorities.

Kett's challenge

Kett showed more organisational skill and decisive leadership than was usually found in leaders of peasant risings. He quickly gathered an army of 16,000 men, set up camp for six weeks on Mousehold Heath and, in July, was able to capture Norwich. The rebellion is notable for the discipline which Kett imposed, electing a governing council and maintaining law and order. Kett also encouraged Protestant ministers to preach to the rebels on Mousehold Heath and to use the new **Edwardian Prayer Book** of 1549. Every gentleman that the rebels could arrest was tried before Kett and his council at the 'tree of reformation'.

The demands of the rebels

The rebels drew up a list of 29 articles covering a range of topics. For example, they wanted:
- landowners to stop enclosing common land
- rents to be reduced to the levels they were under Henry VII
- rivers to be open to all for fishing and that fishermen be allowed to keep a greater share of the profits from sea fishing
- all **bondmen** to be given their freedom
- corrupt local officials to be removed from office and punished
- incompetent priests to be removed from their churches, particularly those who were unable to preach.

In spite of repeated warnings by the government that subjects should not take the law into their own hands, Kett and his fellow protestors pressed on regardless. They believed that the King and Somerset would not only recognise the justice of their cause but would settle their demands amicably. They did not appreciate the fact that no government could tolerate rebellious conduct, no matter how justifiable the cause. To allow the rebels to go unpunished would encourage others to follow suit and rise up against their masters.

Simple essay style **a**

Below is a sample exam question. Use your own knowledge and the information on the opposite page to produce a plan for this question. Choose four general points and provide three pieces of specific information to support each general point.

Once you have planned your essay, write the introduction and conclusion for the essay. The introduction should list the points to be discussed in the essay. The conclusion should summarise the key points and justify which point was the most important.

> 'The main reason for the outbreak of protest and rebellion in 1549 was the anger caused by cruel and unsympathetic landlords.' How far do you agree with this statement?

 ## Eliminate irrelevance

Below are a sample exam question and a paragraph written in answer to this question. Read the paragraph and identify parts of the paragraph that are not directly relevant to the question. Draw a line through the information that is irrelevant and justify your deletions in the margin.

> How accurate is it to say that Kett posed a serious threat to Somerset and the royal government in 1549?

There is no doubt that Kett posed a serious threat to Somerset and the royal government. He was a tanner and was well versed in business and economics. He was well organised and proved to be a charismatic and inspirational leader. He commanded a rebel army some 16,000 strong, which vastly outnumbered the royal troops sent against him. Kett believed that Somerset would understand the reasons for the rebellion and would resolve the complaints of the rebels. Kett was a local man with a good knowledge of the region, which helped with his planning. Kett's march to and taking of Norwich was a significant act because it challenged the government to react either with force or with concessions. Throughout the rebellion Kett claimed to be a good citizen and he pledged his loyalty to the King. Edward VI was but a boy of 11 at the time, with no real understanding of the scale or seriousness of the emergency in East Anglia.

Leaders in challenge: Kett

Robert Kett (1492–1549)

Robert Kett was a tanner by trade and a man of some wealth who lived in Wymondham. Tanning was a lucrative trade and it has been estimated that Kett had property worth in excess of £600 (£185,000 today). Kett also had a number of landholdings which he was in the process of increasing by means of purchase and enclosure. However, he was also guilty of attempting to enclose additional common lands by claiming ownership of them. For this enclosure he was prosecuted at Wymondham manorial court.

Kett was among the wealthiest members of his community. This suggests that prior to the rebellion he was a man of substance and authority within the local community.

Kett's role in the rising

Trouble began in May 1549 with sporadic attacks on local enclosers. The attacks escalated and spread as more and more people became involved. Among the enclosers attacked was John Flowerdew, a wealthy lawyer who was unpopular because he had acquired and partially demolished Wymondham Abbey at the time of the dissolution.

Kett had opposed Flowerdew's acquisition of the monastery and the two men became embroiled in a bitter feud. When protestors turned up to destroy Flowerdew's enclosures in early July he paid them to attack Kett and pull down his enclosures. Confronted by an armed mob outside his home, Kett agreed to the destruction of his enclosures and offered himself as their leader.

He proved to be an inspirational leader who commanded respect. He quickly organised the protesters and actively tried to recruit more followers. Within days Kett's followers numbered over 10,000, then swelled to over 16,000 as he led the protesters on a march towards Norwich. The town was taken without a fight.

Kett's leadership

Under Kett's leadership the rebels were disciplined and well organised. He issued written warrants for:

- the collection of food supplies and weapons
- the destruction of enclosures
- the detention of local gentry.

Kett was instrumental in establishing a council which drew up a list of grievances focused on the rights of commoners and tenant farmers. Kett was also said to have dispensed justice beneath a tree on Mousehold Heath, which came to be called the 'tree of reformation'.

His refusal of a royal pardon and the defeat of a royal army commanded by the Marquis of Northampton at the end of July marked a turning point in the rebellion. The arrival of another royal army in late August, under the command of **John Dudley**, Earl of Warwick, led to Kett's defeat after a bitterly contested battle.

Kett was captured the day after the battle. He and his brother William were taken as prisoners to the Tower of London. In November both were tried and found guilty of treason. Kett was hanged from the walls of Norwich Castle in December, while his brother was hanged from the steeple of Wymondham church.

Qualify your judgement

Below is a sample exam question with an accompanying source. Having read the question and the source, complete the following activity.

Assess Kett's leadership of his troops at Dussindale and the reasons for their defeat. Explain your answer, using the source, the information given about its origin and your own knowledge about the historical context.

Below are three judgements about the value of Source 1 to a historian investigating Kett's leadership of his troops at Dussindale and the reasons for their defeat. Circle the judgement that best describes the value of the source, and explain why it is the best.

1 Source 1 is valuable to a historian investigating the quality of Kett's leadership and the reasons why his rebel army was defeated at Dussindale because it is a personal account, and the person who wrote it may have been an eyewitness.

2 Source 1 is unreliable to a historian because it is biased.

3 Source 1 is partially valuable to a historian investigating the quality of Kett's leadership and the reasons why his rebel army were defeated at Dussindale, because it gives a series of reasons why some of the rebels lost heart and fled the battlefield whilst others stayed and resisted. However, Source 1 is not wholly useful because it only describes the battle from the point of view of the government forces sent to defeat Kett. The source is limited as it does not offer the viewpoint of either Kett or anyone on the rebel side.

SOURCE 1

From an account of the Kett rebellion written by Nicholas Sotherton, who may have been the brother of Thomas Sotherton, a member of the city council in 1549 and later MP for and Mayor of Norwich.

It was a trying time for Kett: the good discipline of the troops that had come against him; the large number of the Earl's forces and the conviction that must have forced itself upon his mind, that his own disorderly followers could not hope to prevail, or that if they did, other and still better troops would undoubtedly be found by the King and his Council. All these, as he looked around, as the battle raged yet more and more fiercely, as the shouts of the victorious troops burst upon his ear, and his followers were fleeing on every side, led him to flee himself: and bitter are the words of Neville as he describes this want of courage on the part of Kett: 'As he had been a bold leader in wicked-ness, so he showed himself a cowardly commander on the battle field, for when he saw everything going against him, the ranks broken, his men driven asunder, whilst our forces were fiercely bearing down upon them, that there was no hope either of safety or aid, being perplexed in mind, and agitated by the consciousness of his exceeding villainy, he decided on flight, he secretly fled from the battle field.'

As soon as this became known, the spirit of the rebels was broken. At first they murmured and secretly complained, then they cried out and at last they began to run away on every side. Our horsemen followed swiftly, and made a great slaughter, for there were slain about three thousand and five hundred, and a great many wounded. The rebels perceiving this, and believing all hope of pardon to be utterly taken away, they urged each other, in that hour of despair, to die boldly, as die they must. With obstinate courage they presently recovered themselves by companies from their flight, and showed plainly they intended to renew the battle, affirming 'That they had rather die manfully in fight, than flying, to be slain like sheep'. After, when they had armed themselves with swords and other weapons, which lay scattered upon the ground, everywhere among the heaps of the dead bodies and so arranged their carts and carriages as to form a secure and excellent barricade. They swore, either to other, to spend in that place their lives manfully, or else at the length to get the victory.

Leaders in suppression: Somerset and Warwick

Somerset

Somerset's leadership qualities have often been questioned, both in his own time and subsequently by historians. Contemporary critics disliked his ambition and his dictatorial conduct in government. They were especially critical of his policy making and inconsistency in his application of policies. For example, although he pursued a programme of social and agrarian reform in areas which included price inflation, depopulation and social injustice, he was responsible for some of the harshest legislation ever passed against so-called vagrants.

Nevertheless, he was hailed as a hero by the protestors in East Anglia for attempting to stamp out enclosure. This convinced them and their leader, Kett, that their actions would be understood and dealt with sympathetically. In the warrants issued by Kett he referred to himself and his followers as the King's 'friends and deputies'.

Somerset's handling of the rebellion

The outbreak and spread of riots and rebellion in 1548–49 caught Somerset by surprise. The Lord Protector was faced by the most geographically extensive English risings of the sixteenth century. His initial reaction was to follow the example of Henry VIII and crush the rebels, but he later changed his mind.

- He publicly expressed sympathy for the rebels.
- He offered them pardons on the condition that they dispersed and returned home.
- He offered to call a parliament so that their grievances could be aired and discussed.
- He set up a new enclosure commission.

However, Somerset's policies angered his fellow **privy councillors** because he had failed to consult them. After the surrender of Norwich, Somerset was pressurised into dispatching a small but well-armed force, commanded by the Marquis of Northampton. Northampton's failure to defeat the rebels led to a larger army being sent, led by the Earl of Warwick. Warwick occupied Norwich and then crushed the rebels in battle at Dussindale.

Warwick

John Dudley, Earl of Warwick, was a member of Edward VI's Privy Council. Unlike Somerset, he was a gifted politician and an able military leader and tactician. He tried to achieve consensus in his political dealings with his fellow privy councillors. Whereas Somerset's autocratic style of government made enemies, Warwick's more open and consensual conduct made him powerful friends.

Warwick's handling of the rebellion

Somerset's indecision and failure to deal with the rebellion enabled Warwick to take advantage of the situation. In fact, it was Somerset who turned to Warwick for help and appointed him to command the second army sent against the rebels.

Warwick planned his campaign with care and precision. He took Norwich and then moved against the rebels camped outside the city. He was helped by Kett's error in moving his force from the high ground of Mousehold Heath to the less defensible Dussindale. It was here, on 27 August 1549, that Warwick defeated the rebels and captured their leader, Robert Kett. With an army at his back and a victory to his name, Warwick moved against Somerset. By October Warwick had replaced Somerset as head of the government.

Select the detail

Below is an exam-style question with the accompanying source and three claims that you could make when answering the question. Read the claims and then select quotes from the source to support them. Remember to keep the quotes short as sometimes a few words embedded in a sentence are all you need to support your claims.

Assess the value of the source for revealing Paget's attitude towards Somerset's rule, and the condition of England in 1549. Explain your answer, using the source, the information given about its origin and your own knowledge about the historical context.

Somerset did not listen to the advice of his Council

_____

Somerset's rule was weak

_____

Source 1 is valuable to a historian for Paget's attitude towards Somerset's rule and the condition of England in 1549 because

_____

Source 1 is valuable to a historian for revealing the privy councillors' attitudes towards Somerset because

_____

SOURCE 1

From a letter written by Sir William Paget to Protector Somerset on 7 July 1549. Sir William Paget was a member of the Privy Council and controller of Edward VI's household.

I told your Grace the truth and was not believed: well, now your Grace sees it what have you to say your Grace? The king's subjects are out of all discipline, out of obedience, caring neither for protector nor king and much less for any other royal official. And what is the cause? Your own levity, your softness, your intention to be good to the poor. I know and understand your good meaning and honest nature but I say, sir, it is a great pity (as the common proverb goes in a warm summer) that ever fair weather should do harm. It is a pity that your gentleness should be taken advantage of by so great an evil as is now in England by these rebels.

Consider, I beseech you most humbly, with all my heart, that society in a realm is maintained by means of religion and law. Look well to see if you have either law or religion at home, and I fear you shall find neither. The use of the old religion is forbidden by a law, and the use of the new is not yet embraced by eleven out of twelve parts of the realm. Whatsoever attitude or opinion men may appear to have they do so outwardly to please them in whom the power rests. Now, sir, for the law, where is it used in England freely? Almost nowhere. As for the law, the foot takes on him the part of the head, and the common people are behaving like a king. They set conditions and dictate the law to their governors saying 'Grant this, and that, and we will go home'. I know in this matter that every man of the Council has not liked the way in which you have dealt with the rebellious commons and they had wished you had acted otherwise.

Failure and impact of the rebellion

Failure

The rebellion had been a disaster for the thousands who had taken part. The vast majority of the protesters had believed that Edward VI and Somerset were sympathetic to their cause. Their crushing defeat by military force and the widespread repression that followed came as a great shock. They did not achieve their demands and no parliament was called to redress their grievances.

Kett and the defeat at Dussindale

Kett was an inspiring and charismatic speaker, but he was no military genius. He lacked military training and tactical skills and when battle was joined he lost his nerve. Moving his army from the well-protected high ground of Mousehold Heath to the less defensive Dussindale valley was a grave mistake. His ragtag army of labourers, vagrants and farmers was crushed by well-armed and well-paid professional troops.

Impact of the rebellion

In political terms, the biggest casualty of the rebellion was Somerset, who fell from power and was replaced by John Dudley, Earl of Warwick. Somerset's indecision and refusal to assume military command of the armies sent against the rebels undermined his authority. Most of the nobility and gentry had lost confidence in his leadership and when his fellow councillors turned on him he had no choice but to stand down as Lord Protector. Dudley assumed power as Lord President of the Council and took the title of Duke of Northumberland.

Another casualty of the rebellion was Somerset's social reform programme, especially the enclosures commission, which ended. Many landowners had resented and actively opposed Somerset's enclosure commission.

The killing of at least 2,000 rebels at the battle of Dussindale had an enormous social and economic impact on the communities involved. In many cases families lost their chief means of earning a living and some of them became destitute. This increase in poverty in communities already struggling to survive the harsh economic conditions simply added to the problems facing the poorest sections of East Anglian society.

The extent of repression

The government initially resorted to repressive measures after the rebels had been defeated. Kett and the other ringleaders were rounded up within days, then tried and executed within weeks. The rebellion had unnerved the Norwich authorities, who expelled non-residents from the city. However, unlike Henry VIII's savage repression after the Pilgrimage of Grace, Northumberland adopted a more measured response to the Kett rebels. He wished to avoid antagonising the populace for fear of causing another rebellion. Local law officers were instructed to enforce the law and to deal immediately with any attempt to riot.

Establish criteria

a

Below is a sample exam question which requires you to make a judgement. The key term in the question has been underlined. Defining the meaning of the key term can help you establish criteria that you can use to make a judgement.

Read the question, define the key term and then set out two or three criteria based on the key term, which you can use to reach and justify a judgement.

How accurate is it to say that Kett's poor leadership was the main reason for the failure of his rebellion of 1549?

Definition

_____

_____

Criteria to judge the extent to which the Kett rebellion failed largely because of Kett's poor leadership skills:

_____

_____

_____

_____

Reach a judgement

a

Having defined the key term and established a series of criteria, you should now make a judgement. Consider how far the Kett rebellion failed largely because of Kett's poor leadership skills according to each criterion. Summarise your judgements below:

Criterion 1:

_____

Criterion 2:

_____

Criterion 3:

_____

Criterion 4:

_____

Finally, sum up your judgement. Based on the criteria, how accurate is it to say that the Kett rebellion failed largely because of Kett's poor leadership skills?

_____

_____

_____

Tip: Remember, you should weigh up evidence of poor leadership skills against evidence of failure in your conclusion.

Exam focus

Below is a source, question and sample answer on the events connected with the fall from power of Lord Protector Somerset and his rivalry with the Earl of Warwick.

Assess the value of the source for revealing the reasons why Lord Protector Somerset fell from power and the part played in his downfall by Kett and John Dudley, Earl of Warwick. Explain your answer, using the source, the information given about its origin and your own knowledge about the historical context.

SOURCE 1

From John Clapham's 'Certain Observations', which he wrote in 1603. Clapham was one of the senior secretaries of Sir William Cecil, Lord Burghley. This extract is focused on the problems facing the government and the power struggle between John Dudley, Earl of Warwick and Edward Seymour, Lord Protector and Duke of Somerset.

Edward VI, being but of the age of nine years succeeded his father in the kingdom. During the time of his minority the protection of the state was by advice of the Privy councillors committed to the Duke of Somerset, the King's uncle by the mother's side, who then caused ecclesiastical government to be altered according to that of the reformed churches in Germany.

At this time there were commotions in diverse counties within the realm, partly about enclosures, and partly for the restitution of the old religion. The most dangerous of all the rest was that rebellion of Kett the Tanner in Norfolk, which was suppressed by the Earl of Warwick, a man of great wit and courage, having oftentimes made proof of his skills in government. There were also factions among the Lords of the Privy Council. For the Earl of Warwick, by nature ambitious and bold to attempt where advantage was offered, opposed himself against the Protector, who, being a man of a softly nature and easy to be abused, was made the means to hasten the destruction of himself and his followers.

Many complaints about misgoverning the realm were exhibited against the Protector by the Earl of Warwick, who then began more openly to show himself, as having to do with a man weak in action and exposed, in a manner, to the power of his adversaries. Hereupon the Protector was displaced and committed to prison, from whence afterwards either his innocency or the favour of the time procured his deliverance and re-establishment of his former greatness, albeit he did not long enjoy it. For the Earl of Warwick grew more jealous and distrustful of his own safety than he was before, doubting that the Protector might be incited to revenge. The Protector on the other side was persuaded by the followers of his faction that he was to expect no assurances of his life or estate, so long as the Earl of Warwick lived.

The Protector was advised to make a desperate attempt by surprising the Earl and killing him in his bed, but either his heart fainted in the execution or his conscience moved him to desist from committing an act so unlawful. However, the Earl having secret intelligence took advantage of the occasion to serve his own turn, and shortly after new accusations were preferred against the Protector who, being brought to public trial, was condemned of felony and the Earl of Warwick, then Duke of Northumberland had him executed.

This source is useful in some respects but not in others. For example, it is useful for revealing some of the reasons why Lord Protector Somerset fell from power but not the part played in it by Kett; Kett's role is only hinted at. On the other hand, it is more valuable in explaining the part played by the Earl of Warwick in Somerset's downfall.

The source is useful in explaining why Lord Protector Somerset fell from power, apart from the first paragraph. The first paragraph is simply background information which does not really offer any insight into the rivalry between Somerset and Warwick or the part played by Kett and his rebellion. The second paragraph is much better in the sense that it offers more information in context. For example, it states that Somerset was facing serious 'commotions' in some counties caused by opposition to enclosures and the imposition of the new Protestant religion.

> This is an effective, if brief, introduction that focuses on the question and offers an opinion.

It states that the 'most dangerous of all the rest was that rebellion of Kett the Tanner in Norfolk'. This suggests that Somerset was facing more than one rebellion and in the midst of the crisis his leadership was found wanting because it was left to Warwick to suppress the revolts. The source hints that the crisis caused by Kett contributed to Somerset's fall from power because the Protector was exposed as 'being a man of a softly nature and easy to be abused'. It may have been Somerset's failure to deal effectively with the Kett rebellion that led to the formation of 'factions among the Lords of the Privy Council'.

This paragraph offers a good discussion of the content of the extract while providing appropriate quoted passages. It also offers an explanation and refers back to the question, and offers some context to the circumstances surrounding the battle.

The source is especially valuable in explaining Warwick's role in Somerset's downfall. For example, the author states that Warwick, 'by nature ambitious and bold to attempt where advantage was offered, opposed himself against the Protector'. Clearly, Warwick was an opportunist who took advantage of the chaos that ensued during the Kett rebellion to destroy Somerset. The source is also useful in highlighting Somerset's weaknesses which help explain why he fell from power. For example, Somerset was not only a man of 'softly nature' and 'easy to abuse', he was also 'a man weak in action' who could be easily 'persuaded by the followers of his faction'. When it came to taking his revenge on Warwick for removing him from power Somerset lacked the ruthlessness necessary to succeed. When presented with the opportunity to kill Warwick, Somerset's 'heart fainted in the execution or his conscience moved him to desist'. Warwick showed no such weakness because when it came to ridding himself of Somerset he did not hesitate. Putting Somerset on trial and then having him executed showed how ruthless he was.

This paragraph provides some attempt to evaluate within a wider context.

Although this source is useful for understanding some of the reasons why Somerset fell from power, it could be argued that it does not provide a full picture of what happened during and after the crisis caused by the Kett rebellion. For example, the author of the source does no more than suggest that Kett's Rebellion was the primary cause of Somerset's fall. Had Warwick and the members of the Privy Council been plotting to oust Somerset before Kett's rebellion – or did they do so only when he failed to measure up to the crisis?

This paragraph attempts to deal with the second enquiry though the explanation is not as sure or confident as in the first enquiry. There is weak substantiation of the evaluation.

The source is based on opinion rather than fact, so cannot reveal the full extent of the issues affecting Somerset, Kett and Warwick at the time. Its nature as an opinion-based source makes it ideal for understanding Somerset and Warwick's behaviour and attitudes, but it does not reveal enough about the Kett rebellion and the chaos that ensued when it broke out or why Somerset failed to lead the army against the rebels. Had he done so, it is possible that he would not have fallen from power.

This paragraph is rather weak and does not fully explore the factors that might clarify the statements made in the main body of the answer.

This is a good answer. The candidate engages with the question and attempts to analyse the source material though it is clear that the treatment of the two enquiries is somewhat uneven. There is some evaluation but also a lack of development in places. The candidate does offer a valid, if limited, conclusion.

> **Reverse engineering**
>
> Read the essay and the comments and try to work out the general points of the plan used to write the essay. Once you have done this, note down the specific examples used to support each general point.

4 Queen takes queen? The Revolt of the Northern Earls, 1569–70

The causes of the revolt

The Northern Rebellion used to be seen as a religious rising, but historians now question this. The rebel leaders, the Earl of Northumberland and the Earl of Westmorland, had genuine religious concerns regarding the influence of Protestantism in the Church. They were especially unhappy with the **Church Settlement** passed in 1559, which restored royal control over the Church of England. But although religion played a part in their rebellion, the earls were mainly concerned about politics and the succession.

The roots of the rebellion can be found in the politics and factions of the day. The arrival in England of the fugitive Mary, Queen of Scots, provided a focus for the discontented northern nobility.

Politics and factions

The first few years of Elizabeth's reign witnessed a period of political unity, when the regime was being established. **Sir William Cecil** was talented and imaginative and enjoyed a close working relationship with Elizabeth, who relied on him for advice. This gave Cecil unrivalled political prominence at Court and made him a target for rival factions. As Elizabeth's chief minister, Cecil was responsible for co-ordinating the implementation of most policy decisions at home and abroad.

Cecil's rivals

Cecil had rivals at Court, but they were never outright enemies determined to cause his ruin. Faction fighting at the Court of Elizabeth did not become a serious issue until later in her reign, when England went to war with Spain in 1585. Self-interest and short-term aims often pushed rival factions together. Cecil's chief rival at Court was the Queen's favourite, **Robert Dudley**, Earl of Leicester. That said, Cecil and Leicester sometimes found themselves on the same side and even when both were enemies neither wished to see the other executed, only 'cowed' or 'retired'. The Earls of Northumberland and Westmorland were excluded from high office and their influence at Court was minimal. They lent their support to another faction at Court led by Thomas Howard, Duke of Norfolk.

The Northern Earls

The conspiracy that led to the Northern Rebellion involved the pro-Catholic Earls of Northumberland and Westmorland. The earls, along with Lord Dacre, had been sidelined by the Elizabethan regime, which did not fully trust them. Aware of the lingering sympathy for Catholicism that existed in the north, Elizabeth opted to put men she trusted in positions of authority in the region.

- The Queen's cousin, Lord Hunsdon, was put in charge of Berwick and half of the border region.
- The Earl of Sussex was appointed President of the **Council of the North** in York.
- James Pilkington, a southerner and an enthusiastic Protestant, was appointed Bishop of Durham.

The local clergy resented being passed over for offices which they considered to be traditionally theirs by right. This resentment was turned to outright anger by Pilkington's aggressive, evangelical style of preaching Protestantism in the north.

! Mind map

Use the information on the page opposite to add detail to the mind map below to show the causes of the Rebellion of the Northern Earls.

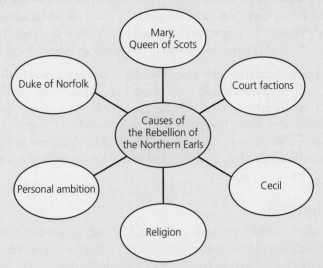

Mary, Queen of Scots — Court factions — Cecil — Religion — Personal ambition — Duke of Norfolk

Causes of the Rebellion of the Northern Earls

i You're the examiner a

Below is a sample exam question and a paragraph written in answer to this question. Read the paragraph and the mark scheme provided on pages 111–12. Decide which level you would award the paragraph. Write the level below, along with a justification for your choice.

How accurate is it to say that the treatment of Mary, Queen of Scots, in the years 1568 and 1569 was the main cause of the Northern Rebellion?

The Northern Revolt was the most serious rebellion faced by Elizabeth during her reign. It was instigated, organised and led by two disgruntled Earls, Westmorland and Northumberland. These Earls had long been powerful in the north and respected at Court but they were increasingly being sidelined by Elizabeth. The Queen did not trust them because of their adherence to the Catholic faith and she disliked their arrogance in assuming that she would reappoint them to positions of power in the north. However, the spark that brought this rebellion to life was the detention and treatment of Mary, Queen of Scots. Defeated in the civil war north of the border, Mary had fled south in search of safety and when she arrived she sought political asylum. The Earls believed that Elizabeth's detention of her Scottish cousin was unfair and unjustified. They also shared Mary's religion and much preferred her as queen to the Protestant Elizabeth. Being northern landowners, the Earls were familiar with Scottish affairs and were known to Mary. They saw this as the perfect opportunity to challenge Elizabeth because they now had an alternative queen to put on the throne.

Level: ☐

Mark: ☐

Reason for choosing this level and this mark:

_____

_____

Mary, Queen of Scots

Mary Stuart's claim to the English throne

Mary Stuart was directly descended from Henry VII and, as such, was Elizabeth's closest living relative. Mary had been married three times and had a son and heir. Elizabeth was reluctant to recognise her cousin as her heir because she might yet marry and have a son of her own. So long as Mary remained in Scotland, she could be largely ignored by Elizabeth and her councillors.

However, while Elizabeth remained unmarried she was vulnerable, a fact made clear in the succession crisis of 1562, when she contracted smallpox. Without a named successor, her death might have plunged the nation into conflict – it was only her recovery from the disease that averted the crisis. Her natural successor, Mary, Queen of Scots, was viewed with suspicion because she was a devout Roman Catholic with strong ties to France. Mary's succession would not only imperil the religious settlement and the establishment of the Anglican Church but would likely be opposed by the largely Protestant nobility.

Mary's arrival in England

This changed in 1568, when Mary was forced to abdicate her throne and flee south to England in search of shelter and protection. Mary's rule in Scotland had been a disaster and her arrival on English soil began a political crisis that would not be resolved for nearly 20 years.

She was considered a dangerous threat to Elizabeth and the Tudor regime. English Catholics who distrusted Elizabeth and opposed her Protestant reform of the Church saw Mary as a realistic candidate for the English Crown. The detention and subsequent treatment of Mary, Queen of Scots, on her arrival in England acted as a catalyst for rebellion.

Plots and rebellion

Mary's captivity in England after 1568 enabled plots against Elizabeth to be woven around the Scottish Queen. The most serious were those involving the Duke of Norfolk and the Earls of Northumberland and Westmorland.

The Norfolk plot

The highly ambitious but indiscreet Duke of Norfolk resented Elizabeth's patronage of and trust in Sir William Cecil. Norfolk believed that he should be among Elizabeth's leading privy councillors. Norfolk's plan to secure control of the Crown by marrying Mary, Queen of Scots, led to his arrest for treason and the collapse of his faction at Court.

Economic and religious insecurities of the northern nobility

The north of England, which was religiously conservative and economically disadvantaged compared to the south, witnessed one of the most serious rebellions of Elizabeth's reign. The Northern Rebellion (also known as the Rebellion of the Northern Earls) was motivated by political and religious frustrations. The Earls resented being marginalised at Court and had never truly accepted the Church Settlement of 1559, which they regarded as being too Protestant.

Moving from assertion to argument · a

Below are a sample exam question and a series of assertions. Read the exam question and then add a justification to each of the assertions to turn it into an argument.

How far was the detention of Mary, Queen of Scots, in 1568 responsible for causing the Northern Rebellion?

The detention of Mary, Queen of Scots, in 1568 contributed to the outbreak of the Northern Rebellion because

_____

Mary, Queen of Scots' detention by Elizabeth I in 1568 caused some Catholic nobles to rebel in the north of England because

_____

Mary, Queen of Scots' detention by Elizabeth I in 1568 was only partially responsible for the outbreak of rebellion in the north of England because there were other equally significant factors that must be considered, such as

_____

In many ways the detention of Mary, Queen of Scots, in 1568 was simply an excuse for already disaffected Catholic noblemen to vent their anger and frustration with the government by means of an armed insurrection

_____

Recommended reading

Below is a list of suggested further reading on this topic.
- John Guy, *My Heart is My Own: The Life of Mary Queen of Scots* (2004)
- Jane Dunn, *Elizabeth and Mary: Cousins, Rivals, Queens* (2004)
- John Hale, *Mary Queen of Scots* (2015)

Threats to Elizabeth

What to do with Mary: Elizabeth's options

Elizabeth had two main options on what to do with Mary, Queen of Scots.

- If Mary was released, Elizabeth could either send her back to Scotland or help her get to France. The dangers posed to England by a civil war in Scotland or a French-led military expedition in support of Mary meant that release was not a realistic option.
- If Mary remained under house arrest in England, she could be watched and her movements controlled. The danger was the possibility of plots being laid to free her or the Catholic powers uniting against Elizabeth to demand Mary's freedom.

Although the second option was not without its dangers, it was the one chosen by Elizabeth and her ministers.

Some of her leading advisers, Sir William Cecil and especially Sir Francis Walsingham, preferred a third option – Mary's execution. However, Elizabeth was reluctant to execute an anointed queen because it would have set a very bad example. According to the Great Chain of Being, monarchs were chosen by God, which is why Elizabeth was keen to confine, rather than condemn, Mary. Legally, Mary could not be condemned as a traitor because she was not Elizabeth's subject.

The Norfolk marriage plan

The northern earls – Westmorland and Northumberland – drew up a plan whereby the Duke of Norfolk would be encouraged to marry Mary, Queen of Scots (see page 50). Part of the arrangement was the elimination of Cecil as a political force. He would be replaced by pro-Catholic sympathisers and the traditional friendship with Spain and its King, Philip II, would be renewed.

The plan fails

The plan failed because rumours of it reached Elizabeth. Norfolk panicked and left the Court without permission. Elizabeth feared he might rebel. Norfolk's supporters in the north, his brother-in-law, Charles Neville, Earl of Westmorland, and Thomas Percy, Earl of Northumberland, waited to see what he would do. Westmorland was fully prepared to rise in support of Norfolk, but Northumberland was unwilling. Eventually, Norfolk broke down under the strain. He wrote to Westmorland, advising him not to rebel, after which he submitted to Elizabeth. Norfolk was promptly put in the Tower.

The Northern Earls rebel

Fearing they might be arrested, the Earls of Westmorland and Northumberland rose in rebellion in the winter of 1569. They failed in their aim to put Mary on the throne, but the shock of rebellion frightened Elizabeth and her ministers. The northern rising acted as a timely reminder to Elizabeth and her government that there were distant regions of the kingdom that had not fully embraced her rule or the changes in religion enacted in the Church Settlement.

Although the rebellion had failed (see page 54), it had set an example for others to follow and the threat to Elizabeth continued for much of the rest of her reign. After 1569, at least half a dozen plots were hatched to either remove or assassinate Elizabeth.

Develop the detail

a

Below are a sample exam question and a paragraph written in answer to this question. The paragraph contains a limited amount of detail. Annotate the paragraph to add additional detail to the answer.

'Elizabeth's treatment of Mary, Queen of Scots in the years after 1568 was fundamentally mistaken.' How far do you agree with this statement?

> Elizabeth was faced with an almost impossible decision when confronted with the reality of Mary Stuart's arrival on English soil: what should she do? Ignoring Mary was not an option, as the Scottish queen was now a resident in England and, as a former head of state, had to be dealt with according to her status. There were a number of options available to Elizabeth, all of which had been drawn up by her closest advisers. The first priority was to ensure Elizabeth's safety, followed by a careful assessment of the threat posed by Mary.

The flaw in the argument

Below are a sample exam question and a paragraph written in answer to this question. The paragraph contains an argument which attempts to answer the question. However, there is an error in the argument. Use your knowledge of this topic to identify the flaw in the argument.

How accurate is it to say that Mary, Queen of Scots, posed a serious threat to Elizabeth in the years after 1568?

> Mary certainly posed a threat to Elizabeth because she was her heir apparent, but to suggest that she was a serious threat is going too far. Mary never intended to kill Elizabeth but simply remove her from the throne. Mary believed that the majority of English people would support her because they were reluctant Protestants forced to embrace this new religion by means of the Church Settlement. Norfolk's support for Mary was crucial to her success, for without it she was unlikely to recruit the majority of the English nobility to her cause. Elizabeth's detention of Mary simply added fuel to the fire and forced at least two members of the English nobility to rebel.

The main events of the revolt: the capture of Durham and the siege of Barnard Castle

REVISED

In order to attract as much support as possible, the Earls of Northumberland and Westmorland issued a proclamation stating that the reason for their rebellion was to resist the 'new found religion and heresy'. They also claimed that they did not intend to remove Queen Elizabeth from the throne, though they did demand the release from detention of Mary, Queen of Scots. The pro-Catholic gentry and peasantry flocked to join what they saw as a religious crusade. In all, around 6,000 people joined the rebellion – a fair number, but nowhere near as many as the Earls had hoped.

The capture of Durham

The rebel Earls needed an eye-catching success in order to:
- attract recruits to their cause
- ensure the Crown would take them seriously.

They marched on Durham, one of the most important cities in the region. Durham was not strongly fortified, so the rebels were able to take the city with ease. Bishop Pilkington and his family were forced to flee the city dressed as beggars.

By taking Durham, the rebels intended to establish a base from which to conduct their rebellion, but they also wished to take control of the cathedral. The cathedral was one of the most important in the kingdom. Upon taking it, the Earls tore down all evidence of Protestantism and restored the Mass. They planned to march south to free Mary, Queen of Scots, who was being held in Tutbury – but they only got as far as Bramham Moor near York.

The siege of Barnard Castle

Barnard Castle became a focus of the rebel earls because its constable, Sir George Bowes, an influential local landowner, had refused to join the rebellion. Seeking revenge for this rebuff, the castle was surrounded and besieged by 5,000 rebels.

Bowes commanded a garrison of nearly 400 men and although he organised a stern defence, his biggest weakness was the lack of adequate food supplies. Bowes hoped to hold out until relieved by royal forces but they failed to arrive in time. The siege lasted 11 days, during which time the rebels forced Bowes to retreat into the castle's keep. Starvation took its toll on the garrison – when over 200 men climbed over the walls to join the rebels, Bowes was forced to surrender.

Dacre and the end of the rebellion

When they heard about a royal army of 10,000 men marching north to meet them, the earls panicked, disbanded their army and fled over the border to Scotland. A rebellion which had begun on 9 November ended without a major confrontation on 16 December 1569. All was not over, for early in January 1570, Leonard Dacre (who claimed the **barony** of Dacre on the death of his nephew), rose in rebellion with 3,000 men, but he was defeated by Lord Hunsdon in a pitched battle near Hexham. The Northern Rebellion was over.

The rebellion achieved very little. Apart from the capture of Barnard Castle and Durham, the rebel army did no more than march to and from Bramham Moor near York.

Support or challenge?

Below is a sample exam question which asks how far you agree with a specific statement. Below this are a series of general statements which are relevant to the question. Using your own knowledge and the information on the opposite page decide whether these statements support or challenge the statement in the question and tick the appropriate box.

'The Northern Rebellion of 1569–70 achieved very little.' How far do you agree with this statement?

	SUPPORT	CHALLENGE
The rebels occupied the city of Durham		
The Crown defeated the rebels in battle near Hexham		
The rebels took a heavily defended castle		
The Queen and her ministers were shocked and frightened by the Northern Rebellion		
Catholic doctrine and order of worship was restored to Durham Cathedral		
Mary, Queen of Scots, remained in captivity		

 Developing an argument

Below is a sample exam question, a list of key points to be made in the essay and a paragraph from the essay. Read the question, the plan and the sample paragraph. Rewrite the paragraph in order to develop an argument. Your paragraph should answer the question directly and set out the evidence that supports your argument. Crucially, it should develop an argument by setting out a general answer to the question and reasons that support this.

How accurate is it to say that poor leadership was responsible for the failure of the Northern Rebellion of 1569–70?

Key points:

- The earls lacked the charisma needed to inspire men to rebel and follow their lead.
- The ease with which the rebels took Durham lulled them into a false sense of their own power.
- The earls wasted time and resources besieging Barnard Castle.
- The rebels failed to engage the royal army in battle.

Sample paragraph:

The earls lacked the charisma needed to inspire men to rebel and follow their lead. They only managed to raise 6,000 men, which was simply not enough to confront a well-trained royal army. The early success they enjoyed at Durham filled them with confidence and encouraged them to believe that their rebellion was destined to succeed. However, instead of marching south in search of new recruits with the prospect of freeing Mary, Queen of Scots, the earls wasted time and resources. When the Crown did send an army against them, the rebels fled, which effectively signalled the end of the revolt.

Failure and impact of the revolt

Failure

The rebellion failed because of:

- poor leadership: it was incoherent and aimless – the earls did not inspire loyalty or confidence because they were reluctant rebels, driven to revolt out of despair
- the time of year: by being forced to rebel when they did, in midwinter, the earls could not take advantage of good weather and plentiful food supplies
- it being a distinctly northern phenomenon: the concerns of northerners failed to inspire the people of the midlands and the south of England into rebelling
- the strong reaction of the Crown: although slow to react at first, the Crown's military forces under Lord Hunsdon and the Earl of Sussex were more than a match for the dwindling rebel forces.

Impact of the revolt

The government was ruthless in its pursuit of the rebel leaders. Westmorland escaped abroad but Northumberland was captured and executed. Norfolk was eventually tried for treason and executed in 1572. The Crown was equally severe in its treatment of the commoners who took part in the rebellion. Nearly 800 people were tried for treason, convicted and ordered to be hanged – though it is thought that only around 450 were actually executed.

The rebellion spurred the government into action. The Crown ordered the rigorous enforcement of the **Act of Uniformity** and insisted on regular and thorough visitations. Most visitations went ahead without incident because they were conducted with the full weight of the law and with the authority of the spiritual head of the Church behind it.

A turning point for the Elizabethan regime

The defeat of the Northern Earls represented a turning point for the Elizabethan regime. The regime, along with the largely Protestant Religious Settlement it had established by act of parliament, had survived its first test and would never be seriously challenged again.

In April 1570, following the defeat of the Northern Rebellion, Pope Pius V issued a **Papal Bull** in which he declared Elizabeth to be **excommunicated** from the Catholic Church, and released English Catholics from their allegiance to the Queen. Hitherto, most Catholics had lived quietly under Elizabeth's rule; after 1570 they could all be accused of treason. Elizabeth's response was to step up persecution of religious orders such as the Jesuits.

Support your judgement a

Below is a sample exam question and two basic judgements. Read the exam question and the two judgements. Support the judgement that you agree with more strongly by adding a reason that justifies the judgement.

How accurate is it to say that the rebellion of 1569–70 failed because of Elizabeth's strong reaction to it?

Overall, the rebellion failed because the earls were frightened into fleeing rather than engage in battle the royal army sent against them,

_____

_____

Generally, the Crown was able to impose itself on the rebels by threatening them with superior armed force,

_____

_____

Tip: Whichever option you choose you will have to weigh up both sides of the argument. You could use phrases such as 'whereas' or words like 'although' in order to help the process of evaluation.

Recommended reading

Below is a list of suggested further reading on this topic.

- A. Fletcher and D. MacCulloch, *Tudor Rebellions*, fourth edition, pages 94–110 (1997)
- K. J. Kesselring, *The Northern Rebellion of 1569*, pages 118–43 (2007)
- B. Mervyn, *The Reign of Elizabeth*, pages 166–70 (2001)

Failure of the rebellion and its implications for Catholicism and Protestantism

REVISED

Elizabeth's 'via media'

Elizabeth was Protestant and intended England to become a Protestant state. However, she did not wish to alienate her subjects or antagonise her continental neighbours. Elizabeth's religious policy therefore adopted an approach described as a *via media*, or 'middle way', between Catholics and Protestants.

The Religious Settlement

In 1559 parliament enacted the **Elizabethan Church Settlement**. The legislation re-confirmed Royal Supremacy, set out the way in which the Church was to be run and established the content and conduct of services in every parish church. The Settlement was deliberately vague on some aspects of the legislation in the hope that it would appeal to Protestants without alienating Catholics. In short, the Settlement was a compromise capable of either a Catholic or a Protestant interpretation.

However, many religious conservatives, such as the Earls of Northumberland and Westmorland, never fully embraced the Church Settlement, though they reluctantly accepted it. The arrival and detention of Mary, Queen of Scots, provided the earls with the excuse they needed to reject the Settlement. The failure of the rebellion had serious implications for the future development of Catholicism and Protestantism in England.

Religious enforcement and suppression

The Religious Settlement kept the peace and had lasted the best part of ten years, but in 1570 Elizabeth was forced to abandon her middle way. Her tolerant religious policy was replaced by a harsh policy of enforcement and suppression. There were three reasons:
- Mary's arrival and detention in 1568
- the Rebellion of the Northern Earls, 1569–70
- the Pope's excommunication of Elizabeth in 1570.

As a result of the rebellion and Elizabeth's excommunication by the Pope in 1570, the Anglican Church became more firmly Protestant. Non-conformity was outlawed, non-attendance at the local parish church was punishable by fines and persistent offenders were persecuted and imprisoned. Catholics were especially vulnerable to this rigid enforcement of the Settlement. Elizabeth rejected the claim made by many Catholics that they could combine their religious faith with loyalty to a Protestant queen. Those Catholics who refused to comply with the law were called **recusants**, or non-conformists.

The Catholic Counter-Reformation

Rebellion and excommunication, combined with Elizabeth's harsh religious policy, fuelled the Catholic Counter-Reformation. This in turn led to the setting up of colleges or seminaries in Europe to train priests who were then sent to England to support and spread the Catholic faith. The most famous college was established by exiled English priests at Douai. Several hundred priests were sent to England with Catholic literature to preach and convert. The Government not only banned these priests and their books, they also arrested, tortured and executed them.

Protestantism and Puritanism

For the majority of Protestants, the enforcement of the Religious Settlement was welcomed. However, the growth in the **Puritan movement** suggests that not all Protestants were supportive of Elizabeth's Religious Settlement, which they thought was too weak and too soft on Catholics.

! Simple essay style

a

Below is a sample exam question. Use your own knowledge and the information on the opposite page to produce a plan for this question. Choose four general points and provide three pieces of specific information to support each of them. Once you have planned your essay, write the introduction and conclusion for the essay. The introduction should list the points to be discussed in the essay. The conclusion should summarise the key points and justify which point was the most important.

How accurate is it to say that the failure of the Northern Rebellion had little impact on Catholics in England?

Developing an argument

Below is a sample exam question, a list of key points to be made in the essay and a paragraph from the essay. Read the question, the plan and the sample paragraph. Rewrite the paragraph in order to develop an argument. Your paragraph should answer the question directly and set out the evidence that supports your argument. Crucially, it should develop an argument by setting out a general answer to the question and reasons that support this.

How accurate is it to say that Elizabeth's religious policy was primarily responsible for the Catholic Counter-Reformation in England?

Key points:

- State-sponsored persecution of Catholics was a key feature of government policy.
- Religious conformity was encouraged and penalties for non-conformists were enforced.
- The Catholic Church responded by training priests to re-convert parishioners.
- The Pope excommunicated Elizabeth and declared her a heretic, which encouraged plots.

Sample paragraph:

There is no doubt that Elizabeth's harsh religious policy motivated Catholic activists to plan and execute a Counter-Reformation in England. This was an unintended consequence of Elizabeth's understandable reaction to the Northern Rebellion and her excommunication by the Pope. When the Pope declared Elizabeth a heretic she became a target for Catholic extremists who were determined to kill her and replace her with Mary, Queen of Scots. For the first decade of her reign Elizabeth had tried to steer a middle way between Catholics and Protestants, hoping that a compromise would help keep the peace. However, the papal excommunication not only destroyed the Religious Settlement enacted in 1559 but marked the beginning of the Catholic counter-reformation, which included the setting up of colleges or seminaries in Europe to train priests who were then sent to England to support and spread the Catholic faith. The most famous college was established by exiled English priests at Douai. Several hundred priests were sent to England with Catholic literature, to preach and convert. In the face of this challenge the Government felt it had no choice but to adopt a harsh policy. These priests were arrested and tortured, and many were executed.

Below is a sample answer on the events connected with the Rebellion of the Northern Earls.

'It was the detention of Mary, Queen of Scots, rather than the Rebellion of the Northern Earls, that posed the greater threat to Elizabeth and her government at the beginning of the 1570s.' How far do you agree with this statement?

Mary, Queen of Scots, and her cousin Elizabeth Tudor, Queen of the English, were rivals. They were female monarchs trying to make their way in a man's world. They both faced obstacles in exercising their authority and they both strove to rule their kingdoms effectively. Mary proved to be a disaster as a ruler, pushing her subjects to civil war, which is why she fled to what she thought would be safety in England. Elizabeth was a much better ruler but even she faced rebellion and potential civil war. The northern rising was one of the most serious threats to Elizabeth and her government, but so were the detention and treatment of Queen Mary. In fact, the two are closely linked – some historians have stated that it was Mary's treatment that caused the Northern Earls to rebel in the first place.

The detention and treatment of Mary, Queen of Scots, in 1568 proved controversial. Mary had expected better treatment from her cousin and hoped she would help her regain her throne. Many English people, too, expected Mary to be taken to London to meet Elizabeth, where the two of them could discuss how best to deal with the problems in Scotland. Mary did not expect to stay long in England. However, her detention in a castle far from London and her treatment as a prisoner caused outrage abroad and made some English people, especially Catholics, angry too. It can be argued that Mary's arrival in England provided the spark for the Rebellion of the Northern Earls. Large parts of northern England had not fully embraced the new Protestant faith and many of its people clung to their Catholic beliefs.

More importantly, the two great northern families – the Percies, Earls of Northumberland, and the Nevilles, Earls of Westmorland – remained wedded to the Catholic faith and they resented, and even resisted, the Church Settlement imposed by Elizabeth in 1559. They were also angry at what they perceived to be Elizabeth's disdain for them. They were not made welcome at court and their status and power as the traditional rulers of the north was under threat. They blamed Elizabeth's chief minister, Sir William Cecil, for their poor treatment.

As a Catholic queen, Mary was regarded by many English Catholics as their natural leader, which made her a threat to Elizabeth and to England's national security. The English Privy Council certainly regarded Mary as a serious threat to Elizabeth. During her captivity in England, Mary became the focus of potential Catholic plots to overthrow Elizabeth, which is why some members of the Privy Council, such as Cecil, wanted Mary dead. However, Elizabeth resisted pressure from advisers to have Mary executed. Mary had once been Queen of France so she could count on the support of the French ruling family, the Guise family, and although Philip II of Spain did not support her at first, he did later. This complicated English foreign policy and soured relations between England and the Catholic powers. This became even more dangerous to Elizabeth after Philip II and the Guise family became allies in the 1580s.

However, some historians believe that the Rebellion of the Northern Earls posed the greater threat to Elizabeth. Any rebellion posed a danger, because it challenged not just the Queen's status and authority but also the notion of the Great Chain of Being. No monarch, whether male or female, could allow a rebellion to flourish. Mary, Queen of Scots, merely provided the spark for rebellion because she was already a threat to Elizabeth simply by being in the country. Once it had begun the rebellion took on greater significance because it tapped into Catholic discontent which might encourage others across the kingdom to follow its example

The introduction is mainly concerned with setting the scene but it does link the two parts of the question. For example, it states that the detention and treatment of Mary were the likely cause of the northern rising.

This paragraph provides a very well-integrated discussion exploring the link between Mary, the north, the earls and religion.

This paragraph deals specifically with Mary and the threat she posed to Elizabeth. It is very well argued.

This paragraph provides the counter-argument and explores political causes and factions at court to support the interpretation that the rebellion did pose a serious threat to Elizabeth.

and rise up against Elizabeth. In a widely popular move, Catholic services were restored in Durham Cathedral, English bibles were destroyed and the Protestant Bishop of Durham, James Pilkington, was run out of town.

Some historians believe that the Northern Rebellion was linked to court intrigue to remove Cecil. If this was the case, this would have been very serious. It must also be remembered that England's diplomatic relationship with Spain deteriorated during this period. The fact that the rebels seized Hartlepool, intending to use it as a base for the landing of Spanish troops, shows that the earls were aware of the international situation. Elizabeth feared the power of the great northern families and the threat they posed to her power, hence her swift action in sending an army north to crush the rebels. This, along with the fact that it was thought necessary to execute Northumberland, shows the seriousness of the threat. The final straw was the issuing of the Papal Bull *Regnans in Excelsis* (1570), which excommunicated Elizabeth, thereby encouraging her English Catholic subjects to rebel.

Clearly there are two sides to this argument. The detention and unfair treatment of Mary were almost as serious a threat to Elizabeth as the Northern Rebellion. However, in the final analysis the rebellious earls posed more of a threat because they had an army. Their example could cause others to rebel. It must also be remembered that the detention of Mary caused the rising of the Northern Earls.

This paragraph extends the range of the essay by introducing a number of relevant factors, though they are not fully explored or debated. This may suggest that lack of time was a factor in this essay.

The conclusion is fair and balanced though a little rushed. Nevertheless it is reasonably effective.

This is a very good essay. The range of issues identified and supported in this answer demonstrates a good level of appropriate knowledge. The premise of the question is addressed throughout, with some attempt to evaluate by exploring the counter-argument. There is some attempt to reach a judgement and more could have been done to develop the counter-argument that the Rebellion of the Northern Earls was a more serious threat to Elizabeth than the detention and treatment of Mary, Queen of Scots. The candidate does not fully explore the potential threat of court intrigue but does cover the other key factors well.

Linking factors

One of the reasons why this essay is so successful is that it draws links between the factors it discusses. Read through the essay again and highlight the points at which the factors are linked.

5 Troublesome Ireland: Tyrone's Rebellion, 1594–1603

Reasons for the Nine Years' War (Tyrone's Rebellion)

Causes of the Nine Years' War

Trouble in Ireland was a constant worry for the English Crown. The Irish proved difficult to pacify and they were prone to rebellion if the opportunity presented itself. The Nine Years' War was the most serious rebellion in Ireland in the sixteenth century. It broke out due to a combination of reasons.

- **Hugh O'Neill** claimed headship over the whole O'Neill **clan** and **lordship**. Not satisfied with the title Lord Dungannon, O'Neill sought to persuade Queen Elizabeth to appoint him Earl of Tyrone. He was supported by his ally **Hugh Roe O'Donnell**.
- Sir Turlough Luineach O'Neill aspired to rule the O'Neill clan and lordship. His rivalry with Hugh O'Neill was bitter and violent and led to political instability in Ulster.
- **Henry Bagenal** sought to increase his power and influence in Ulster at the expense of the O'Neills and other Irish clan families. Besides seeking land, Bagenal tried to persuade Queen Elizabeth to appoint him the first president of Ulster. It was Bagenal's ambitions that drove O'Neill into open warfare.
- The Crown's Irish governors, Lord Deputy Sir John Perrot and his successor Sir William Fitzwilliam, pursued an aggressive policy to exert English control over Ulster, which led to intrigue and conflict. The Crown's plantation of Ulster was a cause of much resentment and was vigorously opposed by the Irish lords in the province.
- Competing factions within the royal court in London sought to influence the Queen into sponsoring their plans to pacify and govern Ireland.
- There was bitter rivalry between Irish clans – families fought each other as well as opposing the increase in English influence in Ulster.
- The Old English families who ruled Ireland from Dublin opposed the clans. Descended from English settler families, these Protestant landowners wished to eliminate native Irish power in the only province yet to succumb fully to English rule.
- Spain attempted to exert control in Ireland, interfering in Irish affairs by bribery and promises of military support for a native rebellion.

Support for Hugh O'Neill and Hugh Roe O'Donnell

The support received by Hugh O'Neill and Hugh Roe O'Donnell was significant because it enabled them to turn a rebellion into a long war against the English. It became a national struggle for independence because of the charismatic and inspirational leadership of O'Neill. Within Ireland, O'Neill and O'Donnell managed to heal the rift between some important clan families and recruit them to their cause. This coalition of Irish lords shocked the English, because they had traditionally relied on Irish disunity to keep control of Ireland.

Equally significant was the support the rebel leaders obtained from outside Ireland, principally Spain. Phillip II was keen to revenge himself on Elizabeth for the Armada fiasco – the Irish rising provided an opportunity. He was determined to help the Irish rebels with financial and military aid. He believed that Spanish aid to Ireland would be an effective counter to England's support of rebels in Spain's Dutch provinces.

Quick quizzes at **www.hoddereducation.co.uk/myrevisionnotes**

ⓘ Identify key terms ⓐ

Below is a sample exam question which includes a key word or term. Key terms are important because their meaning can be helpful in structuring your answer, developing an argument and establishing criteria that will help form the basis of a judgement.

> How accurate is it to say that the Nine Years' War (1593–1602) was as much an Irish civil war as a war against the English?

- First, identify the key word or term. This will be a word or phrase that is important to the meaning of the question. Underline the word or phrase.
- Secondly, define the key phrase. Your definition should set out the key features of the phrase or word that you are defining.
- Third, make an essay plan that reflects your definition.
- Finally, write a sentence answering the question that refers back to the definition.

Now repeat the task, and consider how the change in key terms affects the structure, argument and final judgement of your essay.

> How accurate is it to say that the Nine Years' War (1593–1602) was more a war of liberation against the English than an internal dispute between Irish clans?

ⓘ Turning assertion into argument ⓐ

Below are a sample exam question and a series of assertions. Read the exam question and then add a justification to each of the assertions to turn it into an argument.

> To what extent was Henry Bagenal's ambition for land and power responsible for the outbreak of the Nine Years' War in 1593?

Bagenal's ambition for land and power at the expense of the native Irish led to the Nine Years' War because

_____

_____

Bagenal's personal antipathy for Tyrone was a significant cause of rebellion in Ulster because

_____

_____

Bagenal was an ambitious man but he alone was not responsible for the Nine Years' War because

_____

_____

In many ways Bagenal was as much a victim of the Crown's ambition for power in Ulster as Tyrone and O'Donnell

_____

_____

The Battles of Clontibret, 1595, and the Yellow Ford, 1598

The background to the Nine Years' War

The Irish lords of Ulster – Hugh Roe O'Donnell, Hugh Maguire and Brian O'Rourke – suspected that the Crown intended to reduce their power whilst empowering English **sheriffs** appointed to apply English law in the province. Encouraged by two northern archbishops, Edmund Magauran and James O'Hely, they combined to form a Catholic league.

Their plan was to first raise the people of Ulster in rebellion before extending the league beyond Ulster. They hoped that by appealing to other disaffected Irish lords such as Fiach McHugh O'Byrne and Richard and Ulick Burke, the rebellion would spread throughout Ireland.

The outbreak of the Nine Years' War

Urged on by Hugh Roe O'Donnell, Hugh Maguire was the first to revolt in 1593. Suffering a defeat at Tulsk, Maguire went on to raid Monaghan and Enniskillen in 1594. At this stage of the Nine Years' War, Hugh O'Neill was not involved. Having successfully persuaded the Queen to grant him the Earldom of Tyrone, he was loath to risk losing his gain on a failed rebellion. In fact, the Crown looked to O'Neill for help in putting down the rebellion, but he threw in his lot with the rebels.

The battle of Clontibret, 1595

The battle of Clontibret marked the true beginning of the Nine Years' War because it witnessed O'Neill's assumption of power as leader of the rebel forces. In an effort to eliminate the string of garrisons along the southern border of his territory, O'Neill ordered the siege of the English garrison at Monaghan Castle.

The English responded by sending a relief column under the command of Sir Henry Bagenal, Marshal of the English army in Ireland. In May Bagenal's army of 1,750 men marched to relieve Monaghan, during which journey he was harassed by O'Neill's men.

Having relieved the garrison, Bagenal made for Newry – but on his way he was ambushed at Clontibret by O'Neill's superior force of 4,000 men. The Irish under O'Neill – supported by his allies, the MacMahons, Maguires and a contingent of Scottish mercenaries – gained a notable victory over Bagenal, who suffered heavy losses.

The battle of the Yellow Ford, 1598

Bagenal spent the next three years strengthening the English garrison castles in Ulster. He was based at Newry which is why O'Neill targeted the castle for destruction. By 1598 Bagenal's lands had been ravaged by the rebels and the garrison at Newry was under siege.

At the same time the garrison fortress on the Blackwater was so closely besieged that its very survival was threatened. Bagenal decided to send a relief force to save it.

Bagenal's army never reached the Blackwater garrison, for in August 1598 he was forced to wage battle at the Yellow Ford. Bagenal's force of 4,000 men was confronted by an Irish army of over 5,000. In a closely fought contest the Irish, led by O'Neill, O'Donnell and Hugh Maguire, defeated the English and killed its commander, Marshal Bagenal. This defeat and Bagenal's death dealt a serious blow to English authority in Ireland.

ℹ️ Establish criteria

Below is a sample exam question which requires you to make a judgement. The key term in the question has been underlined. Defining the meaning of the key term can help you establish criteria that you can use to make a judgement.

Read the question, define the key term and then set out two or three criteria based on the key term, which you can use to reach and justify a judgement.

How accurate is it to say that the battles of Clontibret and the Yellow Ford dealt a <u>serious blow</u> to English power in Ireland?

Definition

_____

_____

Criteria to judge the extent to which the battles of Clontibret and the Yellow Ford dealt a serious blow to English power in Ireland:

_____

_____

_____

_____

ℹ️ Reach a judgement

Having defined the key term and established a series of criteria, you should now make a judgement. Consider how far the battles of Clontibret and the Yellow Ford dealt a serious blow to English power in Ireland according each criterion. Summarise your judgements below:

Criterion 1:

_____

Criterion 2:

_____

Criterion 3:

_____

Criterion 4:

_____

Finally, sum up your judgement. Based on the criteria how accurate is it to say that the battles of Clontibret and the Yellow Ford dealt a serious blow to English power in Ireland?

_____

_____

_____

Tip: Remember you should weigh up evidence of modernisation against evidence of failure in your conclusion.

The battles of Curlew Pass, 1599, and Kinsale, 1601, and the siege of Dunboy, 1602

REVISED

The battle of Curlew Pass, 1599

In April 1599 **Robert Devereux**, Earl of Essex, arrived in Ireland to take command of the English forces. The Queen had entrusted Essex with the task of bringing the rebellion to a successful conclusion. Essex was supported by his long-time companion in arms, Sir Conyers Clifford, President of Connacht.

Urged by Essex to take the offensive against the Irish, Clifford led a military expedition north towards Collooney to relieve an English ally, The O'Connor Sligo. On his way there, Clifford's army of nearly 2,000 men was ambushed in the Curlew Mountains by a force of 1,800 Irishmen under the command of Hugh Roe O'Donnell. On 5 August 1599 Clifford was defeated and killed, losing over 200 men in the encounter.

The battle of Kinsale, 1601

In September 1601, a Spanish fleet of 28 warships occupied the Irish port of Kinsale and 3,300 men landed, under the command of Don Juan del Águila. The Spanish landing in Ireland and the taking of the port of Kinsale shocked the English government, which had long feared an invasion. The Spanish had been advised to land in Munster by O'Neill, who hoped it might lead to an uprising in the province – he was to be disappointed.

O'Neill and O'Donnell march south

Gathering an army of some 6,000 men, O'Neill and O'Donnell marched south from Ulster to support their Spanish allies. The English, under Carew and the new Lord Deputy of Ireland, **Charles Blount**, Lord Mountjoy, had reacted quickly to the news of the invasion and soon laid siege to Kinsale with 12,000 men. On Christmas Eve 1601, the two armies clashed at Kinsale and, after a bitterly fought contest, the English were victorious. O'Donnell left for Spain, seeking further military aid from King Phillip III, while O'Neill retreated back to Ulster. A few days after the battle, on 2 January 1602, Águila surrendered.

The siege of Dunboy, 1602

The siege of Dunboy effectively marked the end of the Nine Years' War. The President of Munster, Sir George Carew, conducted a wide sweep of the province to eliminate the last pockets of rebel resistance. Dunboy was one among a number of castles that were besieged and taken. However, Dunboy proved to be the most difficult of them to capture. Garrisoned by 143 men recruited by the local Irish lord Donall O'Sullivan Beare, the rebels were ably led by Captain Richard MacGeoghegan. The rebels faced a besieging English army of some 5,000 men, together with a fleet of ships completing the siege at sea.

The attack on Dunboy Castle

The assault on Dunboy Castle came on 17 June after a siege of almost two weeks. The next day it ended with an English victory, but at the cost of many dead. Members of the rebel garrison were either killed during the assault or hanged after their surrender.

Support your judgement

Below are a sample exam question and two basic judgements. Read the exam question and the two judgements. Support the judgement that you agree with most strongly by adding a reason that justifies it.

How accurate is it to say that the Irish defeat at Kinsale in 1602 was the key turning point in the Nine Years' War?

> Overall, it is fair to say that the heavy defeat at Kinsale dealt the Irish rebels a mortal blow from which they could never recover
>
> _____
>
> _____
>
> Generally, the defeat at Kinsale was a serious blow to the rebels but it need not have signalled the end of the rebellion
>
> _____
>
> _____

Tip: Whichever option you choose, you will have to weigh up both sides of the argument. You could use words such as 'whereas' or 'although' to help the process of evaluation.

Developing an argument

Below is a sample exam question, a list of key points to be made in the essay and a paragraph from the essay. Read the question, the plan and the sample paragraph. Rewrite the paragraph in order to develop an argument. Your paragraph should answer the question directly and set out the evidence that supports your argument. Crucially, it should develop an argument by setting out a general answer to the question and reasons that support this.

How accurate is it to say that the Spanish hindered rather than helped their Irish allies in the Nine Years' War (1593–1602)?

Key points:

- Spanish support for the Irish was mainly diplomatic until the very last stages of the rebellion.
- The Spanish army sent to aid the Irish was too small.
- The Spanish commander failed to exploit the taking of Kinsale by remaining within the town.
- The rebel leaders were lulled into a false sense of security by the landing of Spanish troops in Ireland.

Sample paragraph:

The Irish rebel commanders knew that to succeed they needed substantial support from abroad. Spain's diplomatic support was welcome but did not help them in their fight with the English in Ireland. A substantial Spanish army was needed if the Irish rebels were to defeat the English. The Spanish troops that did land in south-western Ireland did so unopposed, but they needed immediate reinforcement if they were to challenge the English in a pitched battle. Tyrone and O'Donnell arrived in Kinsale too late to do any good.

Leaders in challenge: Hugh O'Neill, Hugh Roe O'Donnell and Florence MacCarthy

Hugh O'Neill, Earl of Tyrone (1550–1616)

Hugh was the son of Matthew O'Neill, Baron of Dungannon, and as such had a claim to the headship of the powerful O'Neill clan in Ulster. He was educated in England and adopted English speech and customs, but he remained committed to his family interests in Ulster.

The young O'Neill was locked in a dispute with Sir Turlough Luineach O'Neill for headship of the O'Neill clan.

The Lord Deputy of Ireland, Sir John Perrot, favoured splitting the O'Neill lordship in Ulster between the two claimants. Perrot reasoned that this would weaken their power and make it easier to control the O'Neills – and through them, the province of Ulster. Ulster was the last province in Ireland which enjoyed a measure of independence from English rule, a fact Perrot and his successors were determined to change.

O'Neill's opposition to the division of the O'Neill lordship led him to join and subsequently lead the rebellion against the Crown in 1595. The successes enjoyed by the rebels were in large part due to O'Neill's military leadership and organisation. For example, he was active in:
- raising and training men from within his lordship
- encouraging English soldiers resident in Ireland to serve him
- hiring mercenaries from Scotland
- purchasing the latest military technology, weapons and munitions.

Hugh Roe O'Donnell (1572–1602)

Hugh Roe was the eldest son and heir of Sir Hugh O'Donnell, lord of Tyrconnell. His half-sister, Siobhan, had married Hugh O'Neill, Earl of Tyrone. The O'Donnell inheritance was the subject of a bitter feud, with several members of the extended family claiming the lordship of Tyrconnell. Lord Deputy Perrot sought to take advantage of this feud to weaken the O'Donnells' power by supporting Hugh's rival to the lordship, his half-brother Donal. In 1587, the 15-year-old Hugh Roe was kidnapped by men hired by Perrot and brought to Dublin Castle, where he was imprisoned.

In 1592, Hugh Roe escaped from Dublin Castle and sought refuge in Wicklow, where Fiach McHugh O'Byrne and Felim O'Toole came to his aid. Hugh's experience had turned him into an implacable enemy of the English. When the opportunity came to rebel in 1593–94, he took it. Although he lacked O'Neill's military genius for planning and conducting military operations, Hugh Roe was a skilled soldier and field commander. On the field of battle he led by example and inspired his men to fight with a ferocity that impressed his English enemies.

Florence MacCarthy (1562–1640)

Florence (or Finnian) was the eldest son of Sir Donough MacCarthy Reagh. His claim to his father's lands and headship of the MacCarthy clan was challenged by his uncle. A family feud ensued, in which the English authorities played a part by playing one side off against the other. Early in his career Florence had been a loyal subject of the Queen, but his attempts to seize control of the MacCarthy lands without the Crown's permission led to his imprisonment in the Tower of London.

When the rebellion began in 1593–94 he remained neutral, but by February 1600 he had decided to join O'Neill. In April 1600, Florence fought a battle against the English and was defeated. Not long after he was captured and imprisoned in the Tower – he took no further part in the rebellion.

Spot the inference

High-level answers avoid excessive summarising or paraphrasing of sources, and instead make inferences from the sources and analyse their value in terms of their context. Below is a source and a series of statements. Read the source and decide which of the statements:

- infer from the source (I)
- paraphrase the source (P)
- summarise the source (S)
- cannot be justified from the source (X)

Hugh O'Neill appeared to be reluctant to rebel against the English ☐

The writer of Source 1 is taking more credit for the rebellion than he deserves ☐

The Irish rebellion would fail without King Philip's help ☐

The writer of Source 1 is undermining his brother's leadership of the rebellion ☐

The rebel army consisted of outlaws, beggars and disgruntled exiled Irishmen ☐

Hugh O' Neill could not be trusted because he planned the rebellion but did not lead it until later – leaving others to fight the English ☐

SOURCE 1

From a letter written by Cormac MacBaron O'Neill, the younger brother of Hugh, Earl of Tyrone, to King Phillip II of Spain. It was written on 20 May 1596.

I, Cormac O'Neill, brother of the lord O'Neill, promise truly, most serene monarch, that I will obey and serve (God Almighty only excepted) you alone, nevertheless deferring to my brother who in this realm of Ireland is more powerful than the person who calls himself deputy to the queen of the English.

At this time, the English made the whole of Ireland subject to themselves, save only Ulster, in which Hugh O'Neill and myself live. We were accorded great respect among the English, lest we should withdraw ourselves from their state, or rather tyranny, and attack it as has now occurred. For when we realised that almost the whole kingdom was thus being made subject to the English, I thought that I should choose rather to obey God and you, King Philip, rather than to prosper by fighting with the forces of the queen and by the wealth promised to me.

Those from other parts of Ireland whom I found to be outlawed, I brought to join me as allies. When they had been equipped to fight, I supplied them with all that was necessary to build up their military strength. Those beggarly, untrained and exiled Irish whom I gathered together and enlisted now have been disciplined and hardened in war.

Hugh O'Neill has been possessed of so much authority and glory by the queen of the English that he was unwilling to be considered to be stirring up war lest he should appear to be acting imprudently. He entrusted to me the plan which he had devised a little earlier, using me as his agent. For he was always of the opinion that a regiment of soldiers should be sent by you to help him against the Lutheran enemies who deceive the Catholics under the pretext of peace. In order that this military help should come across the sea quickly, O'Neill has instructed me to write to Your Majesty. For three times messengers have been sent to you with letters, and having been captured by the English, have been subjected to a cruel death. When O'Neill heard this he did not take it lightly and declared war on the English.

Please send without delay regiments, supply of arms and quantities of gold and silver to pay the soldiers along with engineers to work guns. We have many men and are unable to satisfy their need for arms and pay unless you are willing to help us.

Even if all the Irish were to abandon you, I, as long as I live, will not desert Your Majesty. May Your Most Invincible majesty prevail forever.

Leaders in challenge and suppression: Sir Henry Bagenal, the Earl of Essex and Lord Mountjoy

REVISED

Sir Henry Bagenal (1556–98)

Henry succeeded his father, Sir Nicholas Bagenal, as Marshal of the army in Ireland in 1590. He took a prominent part in suppressing the Irish rebellion. He had a personal interest in destroying O'Neill. The two men were bitter enemies ever since O'Neill had asked Bagenal for the hand of his sister Mabel in marriage. On being refused, O'Neill eloped with Mabel Bagenal and married her. His military exploits in the rebellion were significant:

- In September 1593 he defeated O'Neill's ally Hugh Maguire.
- In February 1594 he captured Enniskillen after a nine-day siege.
- In May 1595 he raised the siege of Monaghan Castle but was defeated by O'Neill at Clontibret.
- In both December 1596 and June 1597 he successfully relieved the English garrison at Armagh.
- In August 1598 Bagenal was killed in battle at the Yellow Ford.

Robert Devereux, Earl of Essex (1565–1601)

Robert's father, Walter Devereux, Earl of Essex, had tried and failed to conquer Ulster in 1576, which led to his death from exhaustion and disease. Robert hoped to succeed where his father had failed. In March 1599 Elizabeth appointed him Lord Lieutenant of Ireland and entrusted him with the task of settling the Irish rebellion once and for all.

Essex planned to crush O'Neill's forces in Ulster by conducting a short but swift campaign. However, he had underestimated the strength of the rebel forces and he decided to lead an expedition into Leinster and Munster to destroy O'Neill's allies.

He captured Cahir Castle and relieved the garrison at Askeaton the following month. Besides reducing O'Neill's allies, Essex intended that his operations would safeguard Ireland from a rumoured Spanish invasion. However, it became clear to Essex that O'Neill would not be so easily defeated and that the campaign was likely to last some months, if not longer. Unwilling to commit to a long military campaign in Ireland, he met with O'Neill at Bellaclynthe ford and they agreed a truce.

Elizabeth was furious, so Essex dispersed his army and returned to court. His involvement in Irish affairs ended, but the rebellion continued.

Charles Blount, Lord Mountjoy (1563–1606)

In February 1600 Mountjoy arrived in Ireland as the new Lord Deputy. He was tasked with the government of the kingdom and the suppression of the rebellion. He was expected to succeed where Essex had failed.

He employed **scorched-earth tactics** by destroying the Irish countryside to deny the rebels food. The policy proved effective but it also impacted severely on Irish civilians. Mountjoy's opportunity to destroy O'Neill came in 1602 with the Spanish landing at Kinsale. His siege of Kinsale forced O'Neill to march south with his allies to relieve the Spanish troops. Mountjoy defeated O'Neill's forces at Kinsale and forced the Spanish garrison to surrender.

O'Neill was pursued on his retreat to Ulster, where he was forced to surrender to Mountjoy in December 1602. By March 1603 terms had been agreed between the two parties and the Nine Years' War ended in an English victory.

Spectrum of importance

a

Below is a sample exam question and a list of general points which could be used to answer the question. Use your own knowledge and the information on the opposite page to reach a judgement about the importance of these general points to the question posed. Write numbers on the spectrum below to indicate their relative importance. Having done this, write a brief justification of your placement, explaining why some of these factors are more important than others. The resulting diagram could form the basis of an essay plan.

'England's victory over the Irish rebels by 1602 owed more to the leadership of Sir Henry Bagenal than to that of either Lord Mountjoy or the Earl of Essex.' How far do you agree with this statement?

1. Mountjoy defeated the Irish rebels in battle

2. Bagenal was the most competent of the English battlefield commanders

3. Essex concluded a successful truce with the Irish rebel leader Hugh O'Neill

4. The Spanish army was too small and weak to threaten the English forces in Ireland

5. Essex was a favourite of Queen Elizabeth

6. Mountjoy's scorched-earth policy was cruel but effective in subduing the Irish

←————————————————————————————————→

Least important   Most important

You're the examiner

a

Below is a sample exam question and a paragraph written in answer to this question. Read the paragraph and the mark scheme provided on pages 111–12. Decide which level you would award the paragraph. Write the level below, along with a justification for your choice.

How accurate is it to say that Elizabeth's victory in the Nine Years' War (1593–1602) was due entirely to the military talent at her disposal?

The Irish defeat in the Nine Years' War was due to a variety of reasons, but chief among them was the fact that the English had better military commanders than the rebels. O'Neill, O'Donnell and MacCarthy were competent battlefield commanders but Bagenal, Essex and Mountjoy were better. The fact that the Irish rebel leaders had been trained by the English and had served the Crown in times of peace suggests that the likes of Bagenal and Mountjoy had the upper hand. The English commanders knew their Irish counterparts very well and could anticipate their intentions. The English also had superior numbers and more abundant resources which, in a long war, would eventually wear down the Irish opposition. Elizabeth's appointment of Essex as her military commander in Ireland was a masterstroke. He broke the Irish and forced O'Neill to sign a truce.

Level: ☐

Mark: ☐

Reason for choosing this level and this mark:

_____

_____

Failure of the rebellion and the reasons for English success

Reasons for the war's duration

The duration of the Nine Years' War was due to a number of factors:

- The leadership qualities displayed by O'Neill, who planned, organised and conducted the military campaigns with skill and precision.
- The fighting qualities of Hugh Roe O'Donnell, who proved to be an inspirational battlefield commander. His example set the tone for raising the morale and fighting spirit of the rebel army.
- O'Neill's success in putting together a confederation of Irish clans and keeping them together for such a long time. He managed to heal the divisions between them, and wield them into an effective fighting force.
- The failure of the Crown to fully appreciate the scale of the rebellion. It did not adequately fund or resource the English armies in Ireland until the latter stages of the war.
- The terrain suited the native Irish, who made better use of it than the invading English armies.
- Support from Scotland and Spain sustained the rebels with funds and troops.

Reasons why the rebellion failed

- Although the rebellion spread throughout Ireland, it was centred in the northern province of Ulster. The national uprising envisaged by O'Neill and his confederates never really materialised. The uprisings in the other provinces were not always fully co-ordinated with military movements elsewhere.
- Mountjoy's scorched-earth policy was harsh but effective because it reduced food supplies and demoralised the peasantry who wished for peace.
- The Spanish invasion proved to be too little, too late. Phillip III of Spain sent insufficient numbers of troops and when they landed at Kinsale, the Spanish dug in rather than push out of the port town. This made it easier for the English to isolate and contain them. This forced O'Neill, against his better judgement, to march south to support his Spanish allies in an ill-prepared winter campaign.

Reasons why the English were victorious

- The superior numbers and military resources available to the English meant that they could endure a long war.
- Some of the English military commanders were exceptionally gifted. Men such as Sir Henry Bagenal, Sir George Carew and Lord Mountjoy were more than a match for their Irish counterparts.
- English financial resources were such that the Crown had a greater capacity to reward those who served against the rebels. Some Irish clan leaders were bribed into surrendering, remaining neutral or even joining the English war effort.
- The siege and eventual defeat of the Spanish invasion force at Kinsale was a turning point. The Spanish were reluctant to commit troops and resources thereafter.

! Simple essay style

Below is a sample exam question. Use your own knowledge and the information on the opposite page to produce a plan for this question. Choose four general points and provide three pieces of specific information to support each general point. Once you have planned your essay, write the introduction and conclusion for the essay. The introduction should list the points to be discussed in the essay. The conclusion should summarise the key points and justify which point was the most important.

'The Nine Years' War (1593–1602) lasted so long because Elizabeth failed to appreciate the scale of the rebellion.' How far do you agree with this statement?

♦ Identify an argument

Below are a series of definitions, a sample exam question and two sample conclusions. One of the conclusions achieves a high mark because it contains an argument (an assertion justified by a reason). The other achieves a lower mark because it is contains only description (a detailed account) and assertion (a statement of fact or an opinion which is not supported by a reason). Identify which is which. The mark scheme on pages 111–12 will help you.

'The Irish rebellion (1593–1602) failed mainly because Spanish military support was too little and too late.' How far do you agree with this statement?

Conclusion 1

Overall, there is clearly enough evidence to suggest that the Irish rebellion failed because of the lack of effective Spanish support. Philip II and his successor Philip III made many promises but they failed to deliver until it was too late. The fact that the Spanish sent such a small military force shows that they underestimated the scale of the English forces ranged against them. On the other hand, this might only have been a token force which, if true, would suggest that the Spanish were not really committed to supporting their Irish allies. It is also a fact that the Spanish invasion force was not sent to Ireland until at least seven years into the rebellion. It can be argued that by this stage the Irish were worn out and were on the brink of collapse. Had the Spanish sent a larger force earlier in the rebellion the outcome might well have been different. The death of Bagenal, one of the more accomplished of Elizabeth's battlefield commanders, shows that the English did not have it all their own way. Indeed, there were a number of other factors which contributed to the failure of the Irish, not least the superior resources available to the English. They could employ, train and pay for more troops than the Irish could raise.

Conclusion 2

In conclusion, it can be said that the Irish defeat in the Nine Years' War was inevitable. Ireland was a difficult place in which to fight. The terrain hindered rather than helped cavalry warfare, which suited the Irish. The weather, too, played its part. The Spanish troops came from a hot, drier climate and they could not adjust to the cold, wet conditions they found in dreary, cloudy Ireland. Hugh O' Neill was a fine commander and a good leader but he had once been loyal to the English Crown. Some of the Irish rebels did not trust him. Hugh Roe O'Donnell was more charismatic but he lacked O'Neill's tactical brain. Florence MacCarthy joined the rebellion too late to make much of a difference. Not all of the Irish joined the rebels — many Irish clan leaders either remained neutral or supported the English. This shows that the Nine Years' War was as much an Irish civil war as a war against the English. This was not a race war, it was a rebellion over differences in religion — Protestant versus Catholic. Elizabeth was seen by many Irish people to be a heretic queen who deserved to be removed from the throne. Religion was the main reason why Spain joined the Irish rebellion because it did not like the idea of a Protestant queen.

Exam focus

Below is a source, a question and a sample answer on the events connected with the interrogation of Florence MacCarthy and the Spanish invasion of Ireland during the Nine Years' War.

Assess the value of the source for revealing the reasons why Cecil thought it so important to interrogate Florence MacCarthy and why he was so concerned to find out what the Spanish were doing. Explain your answer, using the source, the information given about its origin and your own knowledge about the historical context.

SOURCE 1

From a letter written by Sir Robert Cecil, Secretary of State and Chief Minister of Elizabeth I, to Sir George Carew, Lord President of Munster. The letter was written in September 1601. Cecil is writing in relation to his interrogation of the suspected rebel leader Florence MacCarthy.

Much has happened since my last letter with news of Spain and the examination of the Earl of Desmond and Florence MacCarthy. For Desmond, I find him more discreet than I have heard of him, but much as I expected of Florence, that he is a malicious vain fool. When I came to examine Florence he absolutely denied that he had done anything wrong saying that he had a warrant to do what he did in Munster until he had recovered his lands. And as for his supposed support of the Spanish he denied it saying that nothing could be proved nor could it be shown that he had ever written to the Pope on behalf of the Earl of Tyrone who was then in Munster. At which point James MacThomas, a witness, did confront Florence and say that though he could not prove that Florence had sent a letter to either the Pope or the Spanish he was there at all the council meetings held by the rebel leaders. MacThomas said that O'Kagan assured him that Florence would join us and that at the rebel council meeting Florence gave his full support. Florence also denies sending any letters by way of the White Knight's daughter to dissuade Thomas Oge Fitzgerald from surrendering the rebel held fortress at Castlemain. To be short, he makes much of sending Tyrone's letters to you (Carew) and I think he will include all his crimes in the pardon the Queen is considering giving him which is why she asked me to write to you.

Of the Spanish plans I interrogated them; Desmond affirms that they meant to come to Limerick in Munster but Florence would have it that they intended to land further north at Galloway. I believe Florence because this is a place nearer to the rebels based in Ulster. In Munster the rebels have been broken and the province is too far from the rebels in the north. And now, sir, to speak of my own opinion of the Spanish, there is no doubt that a navy and army has been sent to Ireland because there is so much news about it. Some say fifty Spanish warships have set sail for Ireland but where they are I know not. Perhaps a storm has met them and they are broken up. I do not doubt that you (Carew) can get some information from Spain and I will happily pay for it.

This source is, on the whole, quite useful. For example, it is particularly useful for revealing the reasons why Cecil thought it so important to interrogate Florence MacCarthy, but apart from hints the source is not as useful in explaining why he was so concerned about what the Spanish were doing. From my own knowledge I know that the English government was very worried about the Spanish because they planned to invade Ireland and support the rebel leaders. Cecil does not make this point clearly enough in his letter to Carew.

> This is an effective opening paragraph that focuses on the question and offers an opinion.

The source is useful in explaining why Cecil thought it so important to interrogate Florence MacCarthy. MacCarthy was one of the most important rebels in Ireland after Tyrone and O'Donnell. His capture and detention was a significant achievement for the English. They hoped to gain as much information as possible from him about Tyrone's intentions and what the Spanish intended to do. However, MacCarthy was only concerned about proving that he was not a rebel, although he does offer some advice on where he thought the Spanish might land their invading army. From my knowledge I know that he was wrong. They landed in Munster and not in Galloway. This might suggest that MacCarthy was giving his enemies false information and that he was still a rebel.

> This paragraph offers a good discussion of MacCarthy with some reference to the wider context. It also offers an explanation and refers back to the question.

Quick quizzes at **www.hoddereducation.co.uk/myrevisionnotes**

The source is especially valuable in explaining Cecil's distrust of MacCarthy. Cecil was clearly trying to gather information about the rebellion and the Spanish in particular but he was also keen to trap MacCarthy. Even in the face of witnesses who claim he supported the rebels, MacCarthy refuses to admit his involvement in the rebellion. Cecil is quite cynical, saying that MacCarthy hopes to wipe the slate clean by admitting all his crimes – short of rebellion – so that they can be covered by the pardon. It is clear that Elizabeth is reluctant to offer MacCarthy a pardon which is why she has instructed Cecil to examine him and write to Carew for any extra information that might help.

> This paragraph attempts to widen the discussion by focusing on the letter writer's motives and intentions. There is a limited attempt to evaluate within a wider context.

Although this source is useful for understanding some of the reasons why Cecil thought it so important to interrogate Florence MacCarthy, it could be argued that this source does not provide a clear explanation of why he wanted to know what the Spanish were doing. It is only from my knowledge that I know that this letter was written three weeks before the Spanish landed at Kinsale. Cecil and the Queen were clearly worried about the news of an invasion and were trying desperately to find out where it would land. Perhaps the reason why Cecil is not clear on why he wants to find out about the Spanish is because he is writing to someone who would know.

> This paragraph attempts to deal with the second enquiry though the explanation is not as competent as in the first enquiry. There is weak substantiation of the evaluation.

This source is based on opinion rather than fact, so it cannot reveal the full extent of the issues connected with the Spanish invasion or MacCarthy's guilt or innocence. A lot of information has to be taken from external knowledge in order to fill in the gaps. On the other hand, it is useful because it is a primary piece of evidence written by a man at the centre of the events connected with the Irish rebellion. The Spanish involvement in Ireland was part of the Anglo-Spanish War which had broken out in 1585 and would not end until 1604.

> This paragraph is rather weak and does not fully explore the factors that might clarify the statements made in the main body of the answer.

This is a reasonably good answer. The candidate makes a valid attempt to engage with the question and does analyse the source material. The candidate is weighing the evidence and attempting to discuss in a reasoned way what can be said on the basis of it. The candidate is clearly aware of the wider context and does attempt, not always successfully, to integrate this into the answer by way of 'from my knowledge'. On the other hand, little effort is made to quote from the source to support statements or conclusions. The candidate offers a valid, if limited, conclusion.

Range of explanation

It would be useful to look at this answer 'through the eyes' of the examiner. The examiner will look for a range of explanations. In the margin, therefore, write a word or phrase which sums up each specific explanation as it appears. Good answers present at least three explanations and discuss each one in a separate paragraph. Also, highlight or underline where any attempts are made to show links between explanations or where prioritisation occurs.

Theme 1 Changes in governance at the centre

Government and administration, 1485–1603

Changes in the structure and function of the royal household

The royal household was where the monarch lived and it was responsible for the ruler's domestic needs. It existed on two levels – below and above stairs. Below stairs, the servants were employed to serve the royal family in the kitchens, laundries and gardens. Above stairs, the royal family lived in the Privy Chamber, a series of private apartments attached to the royal Court.

The Court consisted of a great hall and attached rooms which catered for government business, public meetings and entertainment. Between the Court and the Privy Chamber stood the Presence Chamber, or throne room, in which the monarch would dine and meet people in a more intimate setting.

Wolsey and the Eltham Ordinances

The structure and function of the household had remained fairly constant for more than three centuries but this changed with the advent of the Tudors who were motivated to reform the institution in line with the evolution in government.

The first serious attempt to reform the household was undertaken by Henry VIII's chief minister, Cardinal Wolsey.

- In 1526 Wolsey drew up the **Eltham Ordinances,** which proposed to downsize the household because it had grown too large and expensive.
- It also proposed a council of 20 ministers who would advise the King on matters ranging from the household to the government of the kingdom.
- Its proposals were not implemented until after Wolsey's death.

During Henry VIII's reign the household became an important part of the political system because many of its members – the King's friends and servants – were appointed to positions of power in the central government. The link between the royal household and the government of the kingdom became ever closer.

Changes in the reigns of Edward, Mary and Elizabeth

The household underwent change during the reign of Edward VI because it was dominated by the nobility. The Dukes of Somerset and Northumberland governed the kingdom on behalf of the boy king and they filled the household with their supporters in order to influence Edward and control royal patronage.

The household, particularly the Privy Chamber, changed during the reigns of Mary and Elizabeth because it was staffed by large numbers of women who, ordinarily, had no political power and could not hold government office.

On the other hand, many of Mary and Elizabeth's female attendants were married to courtiers, who could influence the monarchs through their wives. During Elizabeth's long reign the political importance of the household declined, as matters of state were increasingly discussed in the Privy Council.

Complete the paragraph

Below is a sample exam question and a paragraph written in answer to this question. The paragraph contains a point and specific examples, but lacks a concluding analytical link back to the question. Complete the paragraph adding this link in the space provided.

How far did the structure and functions of the royal household change in the years between 1485 and 1603?

The structure and function of the royal household changed quite significantly between 1485 and 1603. The structure and function of the household changed with the advent of the Tudors, who were motivated to reform the institution in line with the evolution in government. The first serious attempt to reform the household was undertaken by Henry VIII's chief minister, Cardinal Wolsey. In 1526 Wolsey drew up the Eltham Ordinances which proposed to downsize the household because it had grown too large and expensive.

During Henry VIII's reign the link between the royal household and the government of the kingdom became ever closer. The household underwent some change during the reign of Edward VI because it was dominated by the nobility. The household changed during the reigns of Mary and Elizabeth because it was staffed by women. Overall,

_____

_____

Eliminate irrelevance

Below is a sample exam question and a paragraph written in answer to this question. Read the paragraph and identify parts of the paragraph that are not directly relevant to the question. Draw a line through the information that is irrelevant and justify your deletions in the margin.

How accurate is it to say that the Eltham Ordinances were mainly responsible for the changes in the structure and function of the royal household in the years 1485–1603?

In some respects it is fair to say that Wolsey's Eltham Ordinances were responsible for the changes in the structure and function of the royal household in the Tudor period. The structure and function of the royal household changed quite significantly between 1485 and 1603. The structure and function of the household changed with the advent of the Tudors. In 1526 Wolsey drew up the Eltham Ordinances, which proposed a council of 20 ministers who would advise the King on matters ranging from the household to the government of the kingdom. The household underwent some change during the reign of Edward VI. The household changed during the reigns of Mary and Elizabeth because they were women who would require a female staff.

Reform of the Privy Council, 1540

The Privy Council evolved out of the medieval **King's Council**, which formed an essential part of government. It was staffed by men drawn from the nobility and gentry whom the monarch appointed to advise him and assist in the running of the government. The pre-Tudor King's Council tended to be large and unwieldy because the nobility were all expected to attend when meetings were summoned.

Edward IV and Henry VII

A change occurred during the reigns of Edward IV and Henry VII because they opted to consult a smaller, core group of councillors on a regular basis, rather than the larger King's Council. In a further development they also promoted increasing numbers of gentry to their 'inner council', who worked alongside selected members of the nobility.

In the past some historians accused Henry VII of undermining the traditional role and power of the nobility because of his reliance on gentry councillors, such as Sir Reginal Bray and **Edmund Dudley**.

Changes in the reign of Henry VIII

The most significant reform of the Council is said to have occurred in the latter half of the reign of Henry VIII. In the opinion of G.R. Elton, a 'Tudor revolution in government' took place in the 1530s in which the King's Chief Minister, Thomas Cromwell, attempted to modernise and reform the government. This was done to great effect in Wales with the passing of the **Acts of Union**, 1536–43.

The blueprint for change was first set out in the Eltham Ordinance of 1526, which was drawn up by Cardinal Wolsey with the likely involvement of his chief adviser, Cromwell.

The catalyst for change

The catalyst for change was the Pilgrimage of Grace, 1536–37 (see page 24), because it posed a threat to the King and his government. According to Elton, the Privy Council took shape during this period because Cromwell believed that the emergency was so grave that a council of trusted ministers should be called to deal with it. Henry VIII agreed. Without the King's approval there would have been no change.

However, Elton's critics reject his theory. They suggest that the Privy Council evolved naturally, because as government became more complex, a smaller council, composed of skilled and able ministers, proved to be a more efficient way of dealing with important matters of state.

The Privy Council after Cromwell

It was only after Cromwell's execution in 1540 that the Privy Council emerged to become a distinct institution at the heart of Tudor government. For example, the earliest surviving registers containing the minutes of Privy Council meetings date from 1540.

The notion of collective responsibility

One of the key features of the Privy Council after 1540 was the notion of collective responsibility. The councillors appointed by the King had equal status regardless of their titles, so that no one individual could dominate the government as Wolsey and Cromwell had done.

In Edward VI's reign the Council became even more important because it effectively governed the country in the absence of an adult monarch. The Duke of Northumberland took the title Lord President of the Council. During the reigns of Mary and Elizabeth the Privy Council developed to become an integral and indispensable part of central government.

Spectrum of importance   **a**

Below is a sample exam question and a list of general points which could be used to answer the question. Use your own knowledge and the information on the opposite page to reach a judgement about the importance of these general points to the question posed.

Write numbers on the spectrum below to indicate their relative importance. Having done this, write a brief justification of your placement, explaining why some of these factors are more important than others. The resulting diagram could form the basis of an essay plan.

> 'Wolsey, rather than Cromwell, should take the credit for establishing the Privy Council in the 1530s.' How far do you agree with this statement?

1 The King's Council

2 The Eltham Ordinances

3 The Tudor revolution in government

4 The Pilgrimage of Grace

5 The role of the King

6 The Privy Council after Cromwell's death

Least important   Most important

Developing an argument   **a**

Below is a sample exam question, a list of key points to be made in the essay and a paragraph from the essay. Read the question, the plan and the sample paragraph. Rewrite the paragraph in order to develop an argument. Your paragraph should answer the question directly and set out the evidence that supports your argument. Crucially, it should develop an argument by setting out a general answer to the question and reasons that support this.

> How accurate is it to say that in the years 1485–1603 the system of government and administration underwent substantial change?

Key points:

- The role and duties of the King's Council
- Cromwell's revolution in government
- The Acts of Union
- Collective responsibility
- The development of ministerial responsibility

Sample paragraph:

> There is no doubt that the system of government and administration underwent substantial change in the century after Henry VII's accession. Henry VIII strengthened the machinery of government by approving the establishment of a Privy Council. The Council was responsible for passing such vital legislation as the Acts of Union of Wales and England, which extended the reach and power of central government to the distant parts of the realm. The emergence of the Privy Council provided the government with a professional body capable of exercising authority over every aspect of Tudor administration.

The changing role of the Principal Secretary

The monarch had long been attended by personal secretaries who dealt with his correspondence and general paperwork. These secretaries were part of the monarch's household staff, which gave them access to the royal person on a daily basis. Chief among them was the Principal Secretary, who took charge of the monarch's secretariat or secretarial office.

Cromwell

In the hands of an ambitious and talented politician like Thomas Cromwell, the post of Principal Secretary became significantly more important. Unlike his predecessor, Bishop Stephen Gardiner, Cromwell turned the office into a political position with the power to run the government. For example, the highest political office in the government was that of **Lord Chancellor**, a post held by both Cardinal Wolsey and Sir Thomas More, but never conferred on Cromwell. Despite this, it was Cromwell, rather than the Lord Chancellor, Sir Thomas Audley, who ran the government between 1534 and 1540.

Cromwell used his position to chair Council meetings, control access to the King, monitor his correspondence and take charge of the royal seal which was needed to authenticate documents and thus make legal the Crown's policies and decisions.

Dividing the secretaryship

Following Cromwell's execution in 1540, the post of Principal Secretary was split between two men, Sir Thomas Wriothesley and Sir Ralph Sadler. This change was most likely in response to the increased workload facing the King's secretariat as government became larger and more complex. Neither man sought to replicate Cromwell's power, which led to a decline in the political authority of the Principal Secretaryship from the 1540s.

Cecil and the Elizabethan secretaryship

It was not until the reign of Elizabeth that the post of Secretary again became important. Elizabeth appointed Sir William Cecil as her Principal Secretary – he outranked the Second Secretary and transformed the post. Cecil was a professional bureaucrat who had served in government in the reign of Edward VI.

Cecil's administrative experience, allied to Elizabeth's trust in him, enabled him to develop the secretaryship. Under Elizabeth the Secretary was a member of the Privy Council and responsible for the day-to-day running of the government. The Secretary also controlled all written communication to and from the Queen, which gave him enormous power. Cecil was the nearest thing in Elizabethan government to a chief minister.

Cecil held the post for 14 years (1558–72), during which time it became a permanent and influential part of government. His successor, Sir Francis Walsingham, held the post for 17 years (1573–90). Following Walsingham's death Elizabeth left the post vacant until 1596, when she appointed Cecil's son, Robert, to the post, which he held for the remainder of her reign.

Simple essay style

a

Below is a sample exam question. Use your own knowledge and the information on the opposite page to produce a plan for this question. Choose four general points and provide three pieces of specific information to support each general point. Once you have planned your essay, write the introduction and conclusion for the essay. The introduction should list the points to be discussed in the essay. The conclusion should summarise the key points and justify which point was the most important.

> How accurate is it to say that Sir William Cecil was mainly responsible for making the Principal Secretaryship the most important office in central government in the years after 1526?

Cover the chronology

Section C questions cover a time period of at least 100 years and require you to focus on change over time. In order to do well in Section C your answer must cover the whole chronology. Therefore you will need to refer to factors, details or aspects of the entire period.

Below is a sample Section C question. Read the question and select three factors, details or aspects of the period that you can use to answer the question. Make sure one comes from the beginning of the period, one comes from the end of the period and one comes from the period in the middle.

Annotate the timeline to show where the three issues that you have selected fit. Make sure you have one in each of the three shaded areas.

> 'The key factor in developing and extending the authority of the office of Principal Secretary in the years 1485–1603 was the ministerial talent available to the Crown.' How far do you agree with this statement?

| 1525 | 1550 | 1575 | 1600 |

Establishing the post of Lord Lieutenant

The post of **Lord Lieutenant** dates from the reign of Henry VIII and was developed as a result of war. It was a military post responsible for mustering and training troops either for the defence of the kingdom or for campaigns abroad. Prior to Henry VIII's reign the sheriff was responsible for maintaining order and for organising the local militia.

However, the increasing threat of invasion by foreign powers with which England was at war necessitated the establishment of a post dedicated to military matters. The post was also a way that the Crown could extend its power into the localities and through which it could exert greater control of local government.

The day-to-day running of local government and justice was the responsibility of the Justices of the Peace, assisted by the county sheriffs. The Lord Lieutenants added another layer of government, but one which answered directly to the monarch.

The Lord Lieutenants in the reigns of Henry VIII and Edward VI

The first Lord Lieutenants were appointed by Henry VIII during his war with France and Scotland in 1512–13. The richest and most powerful landowners in the country were commissioned to organise local defence. Those counties bordering Scotland and the Channel coast were especially vulnerable to invasion. The status and power of the Lord Lieutenants was such that the majority of post holders were recruited from the nobility.

The first lieutenancies were temporary, designed to deal with specific matters such as invasion from abroad or rebellion at home. The Pilgrimage of Grace was a serious threat that required the appointment of Lord Lieutenants in 1536, so that troops could be deployed to suppress the rebellion. Edward VI, too, had cause to appoint Lord Lieutenants in 1549, to put down the Kett uprising in Norfolk and the Western rebellion.

The Lord Lieutenants in the reigns of Mary and Elizabeth

A step in the direction of making the Lord Lieutenancies permanent was taken by Mary, who divided the kingdom into ten lieutenancies, with the post-holders given responsibility for military matters within a defined geographical region. However, it did not survive her death and the commissions lapsed when Elizabeth ended Mary's war with France and made peace in 1559.

During Elizabeth's reign the Lord Lieutenants were commissioned on a temporary basis to deal with emergencies such as the Northern Rebellion of 1569–70. However, she did introduce one significant change when provision was made for the appointment of deputies.

The outbreak of war with Spain in 1585 transformed the office of Lord Lieutenant because by its end in 1604 the post had become permanent. To guard against invasion and potential rebellion by homegrown Catholics in support of Spain, each county was assigned a Lord Lieutenant and deputy.

The Lord Lieutenants had to ensure that their troops were properly mustered, armed and trained. They were also responsible for discipline and leadership in battle, should the Spanish Armada succeed in landing an army in England. This shared fear of invasion and mutual interest in the kingdom's defence enhanced the link between the central government, with the Privy Council at its heart, and the localities.

Develop the detail a

Below is a sample exam question and a paragraph written in answer to this question. The paragraph contains a limited amount of detail. Annotate the paragraph to add additional detail to the answer.

> How successful were the Lord Lieutenants in promoting and extending the power and authority of the Crown into the localities in the years 1485–1603?

> Between 1485 and 1603 the Lord Lieutenants succeeded in extending the power and authority of the Crown into the localities. They were able to do so because the offices were filled by powerful noblemen. These noble Lieutenants were wealthy landowners who wielded considerable influence. However, the primary role of the office of Lord Lieutenant was in military matters. The defence of the realm from possible invasion or internal rebellion was a matter of serious concern. Nevertheless, by virtue of their office the Lord Lieutenants were able to influence the running of local government and thereby promote the power of the Crown.

Turning assertion into argument a

Below is a sample exam question and a series of assertions. Read the exam question and then add a justification to each of the assertions to turn it into an argument.

> How far did the role of the Lord Lieutenant change in the years 1485–1603?

> There were some significant changes in the role of the Lord Lieutenant in the second half of the sixteenth century because

_____

_____

> The Crown's reforms led to a significant change in some aspects of the role of the Lord Lieutenant because

_____

_____

> The Crown's reforms were only partial, and did not affect some fundamental aspects of the role of the Lord Lieutenant in the sense that

_____

Crown, Church and parliament, 1485–1603

Church–state relations

The Church was an important institution that preached, informed and educated the people, while also controlling them by the power and mystique of God-given authority.

The Church also influenced the politics and government of the kingdom through parliament, in the House of Lords and by virtue of the appointment of clerics such as Cardinal Wolsey to run the Government. Prior to the Reformation, Church–state relations had been largely harmonious – but this changed during the 1530s.

The depth and strength of 'popular' piety were significant factors in promoting religious reform. **Humanism**, the printing press and the spread of **Renaissance** learning fuelled criticism of the Church, but it was the marital problems of Henry VIII that were instrumental in bringing about the Reformation.

The origin of change in Church–state relations

The King's quest for an **annulment** of his marriage had a significant impact on Church–state relations, as it involved the framing and passing of laws through parliament that greatly affected the Church. The Pope's failure to grant Henry the annulment led the frustrated King to turn his anger on the Church.

Henry used parliament to force the Church in England to support his case against the Pope. Clerics who opposed him were persecuted and punished, whereas those who supported him were rewarded and promoted.

Between 1529 and 1536 the laws passed through the Reformation Parliament altered the relationship between Church and state. For example, the Act in Restraint of Appeals, whereby citizens could no longer take legal cases to the Pope, contributed to severing England's ties with Rome.

The Church was forced to submit to the will of the Crown and abide by the law of statute. The Church lost its independence and much of its wealth, and also had to accept a new leader when Henry VIII replaced the Pope as head of the Church in England.

The Act of Supremacy of 1534 and the impact of the Reformation

The **Act of Supremacy** confirmed Henry VIII's assumption of power over the English Church. Henry was now in a position to do as much or as little as he liked in respect of reforming the Church.

The Act gave Henry's supremacy the authority of statute law and those who disobeyed this law could be punished under it. Therefore, the Act was significant because it enhanced the power of both the monarchy and parliament and altered the relationship between Church and state.

The Act set a precedent, meaning that any ruler who wished to alter or reverse Acts regarding the Church and religion could only do this through parliamentary statute. This enhanced the role of parliament, which grew in confidence and authority.

The Act of Supremacy of 1559 and the Elizabethan religious settlement

Elizabeth sought parliamentary support to reach a religious settlement that satisfied both Protestants and Catholics. Elizabeth aimed to establish a *via media*, or 'middle way' (see page 58). To ensure the nation's compliance the **Act of Uniformity** was passed, followed by a new Oath of Supremacy. This was an update to the Oath which brought it up to date to fit the new conditions – taking into account the fact that the monarch was a female.

By 1563 the religious settlement was firmly established when **Convocation** agreed to pass the **Thirty-Nine Articles**. Based on the **Forty-Two Articles** of faith introduced during Edward VI's reign, the new Articles set out the mainly Protestant doctrine and ceremonial basis of the Elizabethan Anglican Church.

Cover the chronology

Section C questions cover a time period of at least 100 years and require you to focus on change over time. In order to do well in Section C your answer must cover the whole chronology. Therefore you will need to refer to factors, details or aspects of the entire period.

Below is a sample Section C question. Read the question and select three factors, details or aspects of the period that you can use to answer the question. Make sure one comes from the beginning of the period, one comes from the end of the period and one comes from the period in the middle.

Annotate the timeline below to show where the three issues that you have selected fit. Make sure you have one in each of the three shaded areas.

> 'The key factor responsible for changing the relationship between Church and state in the years 1485–1603 was the role of parliament in religious affairs.' How far do you agree with this statement?

| 1525 | 1550 | 1575 | 1600 |

The flaw in the argument

Below are a sample exam question and a paragraph written in answer to this question. The paragraph contains an argument which attempts to answer the question. However, there is an error in the argument. Use your knowledge of this topic to identify the flaw in the argument.

> How accurate is it to say that the Act of Supremacy of 1534 was mainly responsible for the change in Church–state relations in the years 1485–1603?

The Act of Supremacy confirmed Henry VIII's assumption of power over the English Church. Henry was now in a position to do as much or as little as he liked in respect of reforming the Church. Parliament gave Henry's supremacy the authority of statute law and those who disobeyed this law — such as those who still regarded the Pope as head of the Church — could be punished under it. The Act was important because it set a precedent meaning that any ruler who wished to alter or reverse the Acts passed regarding the Church and religion could only do with parliament's permission. Therefore the Act was significant because it enhanced the power of parliament and altered the relationship between Church and state.

Development of the concepts of sovereignty of statute and parliamentary privilege

Henry VII

The relationship between Henry VII and parliament followed the medieval pattern being one of master and servant. Parliament was called infrequently and only when the King required new laws or money.

Henry VIII

The **Reformation Parliament** (1529–36) witnessed the beginnings of change in the relationship between the Crown and parliament. Parliamentary legislation established an independent English Church by transferring power from the papacy to the Crown.

Although parliament remained an occasional body called when a monarch required either laws or subsidies, a subtle change had occurred: '**king-and-parliament**' became '**king-in-parliament**'. This created the notion that 'king-in-parliament' had authority over the Church but the King alone did not.

Edward VI and Mary I

This idea was reinforced in the reign of Edward VI but challenged by Mary. But even Mary was forced to go through parliament to repeal the Act of Supremacy (1534) and restore the papal headship of the Church.

Mary was the first monarch to encounter significant resistance in parliament to her attempt at Counter-Reformation. For example, a large number of MPs refused to accept a bill that would have confiscated the property of those exiled from England.

Elizabeth I

By reasserting the primacy of the Crown over the Church by statute, Elizabeth added to the growing sense of parliament's importance beyond simply law-making and revenue-raising. After gaining the right to legislate on religious matters, MPs began to discuss their rights and privileges.

The notion of free speech became an issue which motivated some MPs, most notably Peter Wentworth in 1576, to challenge the Crown's right to set limits on parliamentary debates.

For the most part, parliament worked in close harmony with the Crown and although it never established itself as a permanent part of the Government, it had developed a sense of its importance. This was reinforced by the growth in the numbers of MPs returned to the House of Commons. For example, in 1512 there were 302 MPs in the Commons but this had grown by more than 50 per cent by 1586 when 462 MPs were returned for English and Welsh **borough** and **county constituencies**.

! Spot the mistake a

Below are a sample exam question and a paragraph written in answer to this question. Why does this paragraph not get into Level 4? Once you have identified the mistake, rewrite the paragraph so that it displays the qualities of Level 4. The mark scheme on pages 111–12 will help you.

How far do you agree that the status and authority of parliament was transformed in the years 1485–1603?

There is no doubt that the status and authority of parliament was significantly transformed in the years 1485–1603. In the reign of Henry VII parliament was a weak and insignificant institution, but by 1603 it had become more powerful than the Crown. This was partly due to the fact that the monarch was a woman. The Crown could not pass laws or raise revenue without the consent of parliament.

⦿ Identify key terms a

Below is a sample exam question which includes a key word or term. Key terms are important because their meaning can be helpful in structuring your answer, developing an argument and establishing criteria that will help form the basis of a judgement.

How accurate is it to say that by 1603 parliament had become a permanent and essential part of royal government?

- First, identify the key word or term. This will be a word or phrase that is important to the meaning of the question. Underline the word or phrase.
- Secondly, define the key phrase. Your definition should set out the key features of the phrase or word that you are defining.
- Third, make an essay plan that reflects your definition.
- Finally, write a sentence answering the question that refers back to the definition.

Now repeat the task and consider how the change in key term affects the structure, argument and final judgement of your essay.

How accurate is it to say that by 1603 parliament had become an important part of royal government?

The extent of the change in the relationship between Crown and parliament

The relationship between Crown and parliament changed substantially during the sixteenth century. The parliaments of Henry VII were indistinguishable from those of his predecessors: they were called infrequently and met for a short time, and only for specific purposes such as legislation, mainly **attainders** and taxation. This occasional use of parliament continued in the reign of Henry VIII, but changed with the so-called Reformation Parliament.

The Reformation Parliament, 1529–36

This parliament lasted for seven years, though it did not sit continuously, and dealt with matters not normally associated with parliamentary business – religion and the Church. Henry and Cromwell used parliament to legalise the break with Rome. The increasing frequency with which it was called to legislate on religious matters marked a significant shift in the relationship between Crown and parliament.

Parliament did not suddenly become a powerful institution with authority to act independently of the monarch. In short, it was more of an evolutionary than a revolutionary change.

Crown and parliament in the reign of Elizabeth

Parliament continued to be summoned in the reigns of Edward VI and Mary, but it was in the reign of Elizabeth that the institution experienced a more rapid pace of change. Her reign witnessed a growing assertiveness in the Commons. There were two main reasons for this increasing assertiveness:

- The growing experience and confidence of MPs who had sat in a number of parliaments.
- The rise of a small radical group of Puritan MPs, such as Peter Wentworth and Sir Anthony Cope, who were demanding freedom of speech.

It became necessary for the Crown to more actively control the Commons and Lords, by appointing parliamentary managers to set agendas and steer debates away from matters that came under the **royal prerogative**. For example:

- In 1576 Elizabeth issued instructions to parliament restricting its right to freedom of speech.
- In 1572 and again in 1586 Elizabeth forbade parliament to debate the fate of Mary, Queen of Scots, citing this matter as being part of her royal prerogative.

To stifle unwanted debate in the Commons, Elizabeth imprisoned Wentworth and Cope in 1587, because they wanted to change the religious settlement by adopting a more Puritan doctrine.

This is significant also because it demonstrated the limitations of parliamentary powers. The ultimate power rested with the Crown, which not only had the prerogative to summon, **prorogue** and dismiss parliament, but also retained the right to veto any bill or halt any debate as it thought fit.

Only twice did the ruling monarch face a revolt in parliament when a number of members conspired to reject royal instructions or refuse to co-operate:

- Mary faced opposition to her religious policies in 1555, but she was still able to reverse the break with Rome with parliament's help.
- Elizabeth faced the wrath of parliament in 1601 over the controversial issue of **monopolies**. Only after Elizabeth promised to resolve the issue did parliament consent to pass the measures requested by Elizabeth.

There is no doubt that the relationship between the Crown and parliament had changed during the Tudor period, with the latter institution gaining ever greater prominence and powers. However, the Crown remained the most powerful part of government.

Spectrum of importance

Below is a sample exam question and a list of general points which could be used to answer the question. Use your own knowledge and the information on the opposite page to reach a judgement about the importance of these general points to the question posed.

Write numbers on the spectrum below to indicate their relative importance. Having done this, write a brief justification of your placement, explaining why some of these factors are more important than others. The resulting diagram could form the basis of an essay plan.

'In the years 1485–1603 parliament became the most powerful part of Tudor government.' How far do you agree with this statement?

1   The Reformation Parliament, 1529–36

2   The Crown's growing dependence on parliamentary finance

3   The last two Tudor monarchs were female

4   The growing authority of the Privy Council

5   The development of MPs' rights and privileges

6   MPs, demand for freedom of speech

Least important   Most important

Recommended reading

Below is a list of suggested further reading on this topic.

- A. Anderson, T. Imperato & D. Ferriby, *The Tudors* (2015)
- T.A. Morris, *Tudor Government* (1999)
- M.A.R. Graves, *The Tudor Parliaments: Crown, Lords and Commons 1485–1603* (1987)
- C. Haigh, *English Reformation Revised* (1987)

Exam focus

Below is a sample answer on the events connected with the relationship between Church and state in the sixteenth century.

How far do you agree that the key turning point in the relationship between Church and state in the years 1485–1603 was the Act of Supremacy, 1534?

There is no doubt that the relationship between Church and state changed significantly in the period between 1485 and 1603. By 1603 the Church was very much under the control of the state. The reason for this dramatic shift in the balance of power in favour of the state is hotly debated by historians. Some historians suggest it was part of a natural evolutionary process of change that took place over the whole century. However, other historians think it was due to the revolutionary changes that took place in the government and religion during the 1530s. The historians who favour a revolutionary change in Church–state relations support the notion of a key turning point which, in their opinion, came in 1534 with Henry VIII's break with Rome.

The idea of a key turning point is supported by some convincing evidence. For example, when Henry broke with Rome he was declared supreme head of the Church in England, replacing the Pope, and giving him complete power over the Church. The Church was now subject to royal control, which enabled Henry VIII to appoint Thomas Cromwell as the King's vicegerent in spiritual matters. In effect Cromwell ran the Church on behalf of the King. This was a fitting reward for a man who engineered the break with Rome. To ensure the nation's compliance in Henry's assumption of power as head of the Church, Cromwell piloted a bill through parliament which provided the legal basis for this radical shift in Church–state relations – this was the Act of Supremacy (1534). The Act made clear that parliament was not giving Henry the title because he was entitled to assume the supreme headship of the Church, but because it was his royal prerogative.

It may have been a cynical ploy by Cromwell, but parliament was simply used to acknowledge the King's title, which gave the impression that the English people were fully behind Henry's decision to break with Rome. Cromwell was a skilled parliamentarian and he knew how to get his way. As vicegerent Cromwell ensured that the Oath of Supremacy was administered to all religious houses which meant that they could not block the King's order to send commissioners to visit the monasteries. Cromwell was a Protestant, which meant that he was no friend of the monasteries or the Catholic Church. He wanted to close them down in order to take their wealth and give it to the King. Cromwell tried to go further by introducing reforms such as abolishing traditional privileges, for example benefit of the clergy and sanctuary. This shows that the Church Henry VIII inherited from his father in 1509 – Roman Catholic with over 800 monasteries and with the Pope as head – was very different from that inherited by Edward VI in 1547 – Protestant with no monasteries and with the King as head. This strongly suggests that the break with Rome was a key turning point in the relationship between Church and state in the period between 1485 and 1603.

However, not all historians agree with this theory. They reject the idea of a 'turning point' and do not accept that a single action such as the break with Rome was as significant as their academic opponents claim. In the opinion of the 'evolutionary change' school of historians, the break with Rome simply confirmed the way things were by 1534. The break with Rome, which was marked by the passing of the Act of Supremacy, was merely the culmination of a series of events that began in the late 1520s when Henry began his quest for an annulment of his marriage to Catherine of Aragon. Indeed, Henry never sought or planned to break with Rome – it happened almost by accident. As the quarrel between Henry and the Pope became

This is a good introduction that provides a context to the debate between schools of historians – evolutionary and revolutionary theories.

This paragraph provides a cogent argument in favour of the break with Rome being a turning point in Church–state relations.

This paragraph further explores Cromwell's role in effecting the break with Rome and thereafter engineering the changes that shifted the balance of power in favour of the state. More might have been done to provide the wider context by making meaningful reference to Elton's so-called 'revolution in government' theory.

This paragraph provides the counter-argument based on the premise that there was no single turning point in Church–state relations. Here the natural processes of change are championed.

bitter, they each raised the stakes to browbeat the other into submission. By 1534 they had simply run out of patience and ideas; therefore in itself the break with Rome was not a turning point in Church–state relations.

On the other hand, it is possible to suggest that the break with Rome laid the foundations of further changes in the nature of Church–state relations. These changes occurred over a 40- or 50-year period extending from 1534 to the late 1570s and early 1580s. Some of these changes were significant, such as the dissolution of the monasteries between 1536 and 1540, which removed all religious houses from England and Wales. One could argue that if the notion of a turning point is accepted then the dissolution is a likely candidate. The fact that the dissolution witnessed the transfer of the monasteries' extensive lands to the Crown certainly contributed to a change in Church–state relations.

This paragraph extends the range of the debate by linking the evolutionary and revolutionary theories. The argument here could have been more clearly expressed.

If we move beyond Henry VIII's reign it is possible to point to a number of equally significant changes such as the Act of Supremacy of 1559, which was necessary because Mary I had repealed her father's Act of 1534. This suggests that the break with Rome was not a turning point in Church–state relations because the Pope was restored as head of the Church by Mary. The Pope was removed again by Elizabeth in 1559, which might be considered another break with Rome. Her break with Rome and the Act of Supremacy that acknowledged it were much longer-lasting than the equivalents of 1534. The English Prayer Books passed into law by the Acts of 1549 and 1552 and 1559 did more to shape the nature of the Church of England than did the break with Rome.

This paragraph provides some wider context by going beyond Henry VIII's reign to try and cover the period. The candidate is aware of the demands of the question in trying to cover 100 years.

In conclusion, the complexity of the issue is not clear-cut, hence the continuing debate among historians. But one final thought: it may be possible to say that the change in Church–state relations was due to a series of turning points not important in themselves, but collectively adding up to something more significant.

The conclusion is short and misses the opportunity to round off the debate with a more meaningful comment on the key factors. On the other hand, there is a suggested alternative way to look at the issue.

This is a very good essay. The range of issues identified and supported in this answer demonstrates a good level of appropriate knowledge. The premise of the question is addressed throughout with some attempt to evaluate by exploring the counter-argument. There is a limited attempt to reach a judgement and more could have been done to develop the counter-argument. The conclusion is short though it does contain an intriguing alternative viewpoint.

Consolidation

This is a long and detailed essay. Without losing the overall argument of the essay, experiment with reducing its length by 100 words. This is a particularly useful exercise for trying to produce an essay which gets to the heart of the question without being overlong.

Theme 2 Gaining the co-operation of the localities

Involving the localities in governance, 1485–1603

Relations with localities

The regional division of the kingdom of England was marked by councils set up to govern distant and distinct parts of the realm.

- Six counties of the north of England were governed through the **Council of the North**, based in York.
- Wales and four western counties of England were governed through the Council of Wales and the Marches, based in Ludlow.

Regional division was complicated by:

- the existence of semi-independent lordships, which were self-governing units in which the **'King's writ did not run'**. The Crown had limited power in the **Marcher lordships** of Wales and the **County Palatines** of Durham and Chester.
- ethnic differences. Wales and Cornwall had their own language and culture. They did not speak English and were more inclined to follow their own local leaders than those officers sent to govern them by a London-based government.
- cultural differences. Within England there were great differences between regions, counties and even neighbouring villages. For example, Yorkshire folk resented being taxed and governed by southerners, which led in part to the Yorkshire rebellion of 1489 and the Pilgrimage of Grace in 1536–37.

The Crown's drive to forge stronger links between central and local governments caused friction in these distant regions. Regional loyalties were strong and there was often resentment at what was regarded as outside interference. The extension of royal government was accompanied by a strengthening of royal justice. This led to greater control being exerted over local officers such as Justices of the Peace.

Officials appointed by the London-based government were unwelcome in regions where local lords had been passed over in favour of royal nominees. This sometimes soured relations with localities, such as in 1569 when the Northern Earls, Westmorland and Northumberland, rebelled.

Re-establishing the Council of the North, 1537

The Council of the North was established in 1472 to govern the northern counties of Yorkshire, Lancashire, Cumberland, Westmorland, Durham and Northumberland. It lapsed after the death of Richard III until it was re-established in 1489 by Henry VII. After Henry VII's death in 1509 the Council lapsed again, meeting infrequently. However, the shock caused by the Pilgrimage of Grace forced Henry to re-establish the Council as a means of strengthening royal control of the north. Thereafter, the Crown appointed powerful noblemen to the presidency of the council with the express instruction of keeping the peace, raising revenue and extending royal justice into the remoter parts of the north.

The Acts of Union or Law in Wales Acts, 1536 and 1543

Between 1536 and 1543 the government and administration of Wales was transformed by Cromwell's reforms. Lawlessness and disorder were the main problems facing the Crown in Wales because the country was split between Crown lands and Marcher lordships. Cromwell realised that better government would only be achieved through a uniform system of administration and justice.

By virtue of the Acts of Union Wales was fully integrated into the English state. The Welsh were forced to adopt English law, speech and customs. For the first time, Welsh members were elected to parliament and justices of the peace were appointed to the newly created counties of the principality.

! Simple essay style — a

Below is a sample exam question. Use your own knowledge and the information on the opposite page to produce a plan for this question. Choose four general points and provide three pieces of specific information to support each general point. Once you have planned your essay, write the introduction and conclusion for the essay. The introduction should list the points to be discussed in the essay. The conclusion should summarise the key points and justify which point was the most important.

> How accurate is it to say that the main reason for the Acts of Union in the years 1536–43 was the Crown's desire to forge stronger links between central and local governments?

⚡ Support your judgement — a

Below are a sample exam question and two basic judgements. Read the exam question and the two judgements. Support the judgement that you agree with most strongly by adding a reason that justifies it.

> How accurate is it to say that in the years 1485–1603 the Crown had created a stable and successful system of regional and local government?

Overall, the Tudor Crown failed to create a stable and successful system of local government by 1603

_____

_____

Generally, Tudor monarchs were able to create a stable and successful system of regional and local government by 1603

_____

_____

Tip: Whichever option you choose you will have to weigh up both sides of the argument. You could use phrases such as 'whereas' or words like 'although' in order to help the process of evaluation.

Increasing borough representation in the Commons over the period

The Tudor period witnessed a remarkable phenomenon – as the House of Commons expanded the House of Lords contracted. There were two reasons for this change:

- Henry VIII cut the number of lords by half when the heads of monasteries were removed, as their institutions were dissolved. In 1547 the Lords had 84 members.
- The increasing urban population led to a corresponding rise in the number of borough constituencies being created. In 1547 the Commons had 342 members.

After 1547 the number of MPs in the Commons rose rapidly. For example, the number of new borough constituencies in:

- Edward VI's reign was 20
- Mary I's reign was 21
- Elizabeth I's reign was 62.

Some of these borough constituencies were rotten boroughs – villages given representation as a favour to local noble landowners or designed to support the Crown by nominating members likely to support the monarch in parliamentary debates. However, other boroughs were created to reflect the growing economic importance of a particular town.

The increase in borough representation led to a corresponding increase in merchants and lawyers being elected to parliament. An increasing number of borough MPs did not owe their seats to either noble or royal patronage, which enabled them to act independently in the Commons. From this radical group of MPs emerged men such as:

- Peter Wentworth, member for Barnstaple
- Thomas Norton, member for Berwick
- Sir Anthony Cope, member for Banbury.

The influx of mainly borough MPs with legal training did much to raise awareness of the issue of rights and privileges. They were skilled and confident enough to challenge the existing system and suggested areas for improvement or reform.

Impact of increasing literacy in the yeoman class

In his publication of 1533 entitled *Apologye*, Sir Thomas More estimated that nearly 60 per cent of the population of England was literate. This was due in large part to the work of guild schools and Church or monastic schools which provided a basic education for the population at large. The **yeomen** class, those richer peasants who had a trade or land and money to spend, were more proactive in seeking an education. As the world of business evolved and became more complex it was important for this class of ambitious entrepreneurs to understand the paperwork that went with it.

As the demand for education rose, so did the number of schools in order to cater for it. For example, during Elizabeth's reign some 160 new grammar schools were established. This had a significant impact on literacy levels among the yeomen farmers – for example, the literacy rates in the yeoman class rose:

- in Durham from 63 per cent in 1560 to 77 per cent by 1600
- in East Anglia from 45 per cent in 1560 to 68 per cent by 1600.

Literacy rates improved in line with economic growth so that a wealthier yeoman class showed a greater awareness of and interest in politics, government and local office.

Identify the concept   a

Below are four sample exam questions based on some of the following concepts:

- **Cause** – questions concern the reasons for something, or why something happened
- **Consequence** – questions concern the impact of an event, an action or a policy
- **Change/continuity** – questions ask you to investigate the extent to which things changed or stayed the same
- **Similarity/difference** – questions ask you to investigate the extent to which two events, actions or policies were similar
- **Significance** – questions concern the importance of an event, an action or a policy

Read each of the questions and work out which of the concepts they are based on.

'Grammar schools had little long-term impact on literacy levels among the yeomen farmers in the years 1485–1603.' How far do you agree with this statement?

How far did borough representation in parliament change in the years 1485–1603?

How accurate is it to say that the years 1485–1603 witnessed a significant increase in merchants and lawyers being elected to parliament?

How far do you agree that a wealthier yeoman class showed a greater awareness of and interest in politics, government and local office in the years 1485–1603?

Recommended reading

Below is a list of suggested further reading on this topic.

- M.A.R. Graves, *The Tudor Parliaments: Crown, Lords and Commons 1485–1603* (1987)
- Jennifer Loach, *Parliament Under the Tudors* (1991)
- Chris Kyle, *Managing Tudor and Stuart Parliaments* (2015)

The changing role of Justices of the Peace

Justices of the Peace (JPs) became the most important royal officials in local government. They were selected from the landowning elite and were appointed to the commission of the peace for life. They were expected to live in the county in which they conducted their judicial and administrative work. The average number of justices per county rose from 10 in 1485 to between 40 and 50 by 1603.

Judicial role

Justices of the Peace met and dispensed justice in local courts known as **Quarter Sessions** which met four times a year. Here they dealt with cases of:
- assault
- burglary
- riot
- witchcraft
- failure to attend church
- vagrancy.

For more serious offences, JPs sent criminals to the senior courts, or **Courts of Assize**. The highest criminal court was the **Court of the King's Bench**.

Administrative role

JPs were not simply justices concerned with the maintenance of peace and public order, they were also expected to govern and administer the county on behalf of the Crown and central government. For example, they were responsible for:
- licensing alehouses
- maintaining roads and bridges
- overseeing weekly markets
- regulating wages
- imposing poor rates.

In 1586 the Privy Council issued a 'Book of Orders' which set out for the first time in print the duties and responsibilities expected of JPs. It listed 306 statutes they were responsible for enforcing.

The Tudor subsidy of 1513

The **Subsidy Act of 1513** was significant because parliament had succeeded in establishing an agreed form of directly assessed subsidy. Prior to this date, subsidies had been levied on communities rather than individuals, which was unfair. In 1513 Cardinal Wolsey drew up a new system of taxation by which parliament granted taxes assessed on incomes.

The 1513 subsidy was the first major extension of the taxation system since the fourteenth century. The burden of subsidy collection fell on the county justices, which added to their steadily increasing workload.

The Statute of Artificers, 1563

The **Statute of Artificers** was a legislative achievement that marked a change in attitude towards the poor and vagrant. The poor and vagrant had been treated with suspicion for much of the period because:
- The government feared riots and rebellion from idle, disgruntled able-bodied poor.
- The landowning elite were afraid of crime committed against their property.

This attitude had changed during Elizabeth's reign, when it became apparent that punishment alone was unlikely to solve poverty and vagrancy.

The Acts for the Relief of the Poor, 1598 and 1601

The drive to understand and improve the plight of the poor and vagrant culminated in the Acts of 1598 and 1601, which set up a system of poor relief across the kingdom. The Church encouraged charity and philanthropy.

The most generous benefactors to the poor were the merchants and fellow townsmen who helped fund hospitals and schools. The passing of the Poor Laws had encouraged a significant change in attitudes, to the poor and vagrant. By highlighting the plight of the poor, allied to a greater understanding of the causes of poverty, the rich were more inclined to relieve than suppress the poor.

⊕ RAG – Rate the timeline **a**

Below are a sample exam question and a timeline. Read the question, study the timeline and, using three coloured pens, put a red, amber or green star next to the events to show:

- Red: events and policies that have no relevance to the question
- Amber: events and policies that have some significance to the question
- Green: events and policies that are directly relevant to the question

1 How far do you agree that in the years 1485–1603 the role and authority of the Justice of the Peace was transformed?

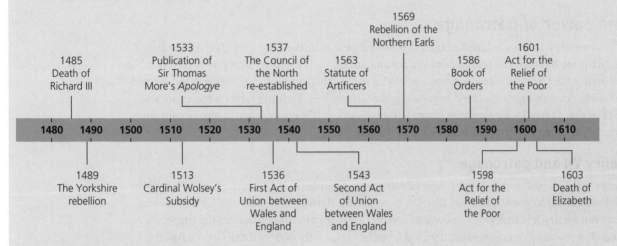

Now repeat the activity with the following questions:

2 How far do you agree that the office of the Justice of the Peace was more powerful in 1603 than it had been in 1485?

3 How far did the power and authority of the Justice of the Peace change in the years 1485–1603?

ⓘ Turning assertion into argument

Below are a sample exam question and a series of assertions. Read the exam question and then add a justification to each of the assertions to turn it into an argument.

How far did the Crown's relationship with the localities change in the years 1485–1603?

> There were small changes in the Crown's relationship with the localities because…
>
> Cromwell's reforms led to a significant change in some aspects of the Crown's relationship with the localities because…
>
> Cromwell's reforms were only partial, and did not affect some fundamental aspects of the Crown's relationship with the localities in the sense that…
>
> In many ways Sir William Cecil did more to change the Crown's relations with the localities than any of his predecessors because…

The Crown and the country, 1485–1603

The period between 1485 and 1603 was marked by the development of a network of personal relationships by patronage. This policy was designed to increase the Crown's power at the centre whilst at the same time extending its authority out into the furthest reaches of the kingdom.

The Tudors were determined to govern every part of their kingdom, no matter how far from London or how remote the location. By rewarding landowners of various social ranks they hoped to bind the **political nation** into a close relationship with their sovereign. In large part this policy relied on the Crown having the wealth and other material resources to grant lands, titles and positions at court.

The power of patronage

The monarch was the wealthiest and most powerful person in the kingdom. The monarch had the financial and material resources to reward and enrich their subjects. This power to reward by bestowing the Crown's patronage was a powerful tool in the hands of an intelligent and shrewd monarch. A weak monarch could impoverish the Crown by rewarding subjects too easily and weaken the monarchy by alienating those left unrewarded. Therefore it was important for the monarch to spread their rewards as widely as possible.

Henry VII and patronage

Henry VII was well aware of the power of patronage. He inherited an impoverished Crown on the brink of bankruptcy. His twin aim was to secure his dynasty and make the Crown solvent. Early on, Henry VII realised the power of reward. To maintain his position on the throne he needed to reward his most powerful subjects, but he could only do this if the Crown had the money, land and titles to distribute.

Henry followed a strict policy of rewarding only the most faithful and keeping the rest in suspension with the prospect of future patronage. It was an effective policy. For example, his uncle, Jasper Tudor, was given the title Duke of Bedford (to add to his existing title of Earl of Pembroke) and office as governor of Wales and the English border counties. Henry VII differed from previous monarchs in that he expected people to earn the right to royal patronage.

In this respect he laid the foundations of a 'service nobility', with rewards given for serving the Crown rather than being simply based on traditional and long-standing titles and landholdings. Thus ancient nobility such as the Howard Dukes of Norfolk had to compete for the King's favour alongside more recently created noble lines such as the Stanley Earls of Derby.

Patronage and the Court

It stands to reason that the Tudor Court was the centre of a web of patronage. The leading courtiers, who were nearest to the monarch, would be the first to receive royal rewards. These might come in the form of money, land, titles or offices. In this way the monarch was able to build up a Court network of dependent courtiers who would be loath to rebel or resist the sovereign for fear of losing their privileges. This did not always work, as the following examples show:

- The Earl of Lincoln rebelled against Henry VII in 1487.
- Lords Darcy and Hussey rebelled against Henry VIII in 1536.
- Sir Thomas Wyatt and the Duke of Suffolk rebelled against Mary I in 1553.
- The Earls of Westmorland and Northumberland rebelled against Elizabeth I in 1569.
- The Earl of Essex rebelled against Elizabeth I in 1601.

Support your judgement

Below are a sample exam question and two basic judgments. Read the exam question and the two judgements. Support the judgement that you agree with most strongly by adding a reason that justifies it.

How accurate is it to say that in the years 1485–1603 royal patronage was mainly responsible for the creation of stable and successful government?

> Overall, the creation of a stable and successful government had little to do with patronage
>
> _____
>
> _____
>
> Generally, the power of patronage enabled the Tudor monarchs to establish a stable and successful system of government
>
> _____
>
> _____

Tip: Whichever option you choose you will have to weigh up both sides of the argument. You could use phrases such as 'whereas' or words like 'although' in order to help the process of evaluation.

You're the examiner

Below are a sample exam question and a paragraph written in answer to this question. Read the paragraph and the mark scheme provided on pages 111–12. Decide which level you would award the paragraph. Write the level below, along with a justification for your choice.

How accurate is it to say that, in the years 1485–1603, the power to deny patronage was the most powerful weapon that the Tudor monarchs possessed?

> The Tudor Court was the centre of a web of patronage. The power to reward was a powerful tool in the hands of a shrewd or unscrupulous monarch. A weak monarch could impoverish the Crown by rewarding subjects too easily and weaken the monarchy by alienating those left unrewarded. Therefore it was important for the monarch to spread their rewards as widely as possible. The leading courtiers nearest to the monarch were among the first to receive royal rewards. These rewards often came in the form of money, land, titles or offices. In this way the monarch was able to build up a Court network of dependent courtiers who would be loath to rebel or resist the sovereign for fear of losing their privileges. However, this did not always work in practice.

Level: ☐

Mark: ☐

Reason for choosing this level and this mark:

_____

_____

The development of a network of personal relationships by patronage

The Boleyns and patronage

When Anne Boleyn became the King's mistress in 1527 she, too, became a source of patronage. Ambitious men flocked to Anne in the hope of impressing her and thereby benefitting from her patronage. When she became Queen in 1533 she also had her own household.

Anne's family also became a source of patronage. Her father, Thomas Boleyn, is a good example of a man made rich and powerful by virtue of royal patronage. Boleyn had come to the King's notice due to his diplomatic service, for which he was rewarded in

- 1521 by being appointed Treasurer of the Royal Household
- 1523 when he was made a Knight of the Garter.

However, it was through the personal relationships of his daughters, Mary and Anne, with Henry VIII that Boleyn gained his greatest reward. In 1530 he gained an important government office as Lord Privy Seal and also the titles Viscount Rochford, Earl of Wilshire and Earl of Ormond.

Relationship networks linked to patronage

Those courtiers in receipt of the Crown's patronage were themselves often besieged with requests for reward. In this way, powerful courtiers could establish networks of support in the kingdom. For example, in Elizabeth's reign, the Queen's favourite, Robert Dudley, Earl of Leicester, was in a position to reward several hundred men who thus became his clients.

This enabled Leicester to extend his influence and exercise some authority in regions in which his client base was strongest. For example, as Baron Denbigh he commanded significant support in north Wales. In Warwickshire and the west Midlands, he and his brother, the Earl of Warwick, ruled almost as kings.

Some of Leicester's clients were themselves powerful men in their own locality but they lacked the essential ingredient of a place at Court. It has been estimated that by 1547 there were over 200 posts at Court and in the royal household that ambitious men could compete for – and competition could be fierce.

Problems with patronage

The main problem with patronage was that there was never ever enough to go round. Many ambitious men were left dissatisfied with their rewards, which bred resentment. The competition for reward at Court bred factions. The more powerful the courtier, the larger the faction.

Faction fights at Court sometimes broke out over personal envy or over issues such as the change in religion. For example, at the Court of Henry VIII the break with Rome and proposed changes in Church doctrine prompted the clash between the reformists, under Cromwell, and the conservatives, under Norfolk. To add to this potentially toxic mix of bitter rivalry, there were other competing factions, such as that attached to the Boleyns and the Duke of Suffolk.

The management of these competing factions required a strong monarch, which was fine under Henry VII and Henry VIII, but in the reign of the boy king Edward VI this sovereign strength was absent. This contributed to the faction fight between Somerset and Northumberland, which led to a change in the government.

Simple essay style

Below is a sample exam question. Use your own knowledge and the information on the opposite page to produce a plan for this question. Choose four general points and provide three pieces of specific information to support each general point. Once you have planned your essay, write the introduction and conclusion for the essay. The introduction should list the points to be discussed in the essay. The conclusion should summarise the key points and justify which point was the most important.

> How accurate is it to say that the main reason for the outbreak of faction fights at Court in the years 1485–1603 was conflict over the bestowal of patronage?

The flaw in the argument

Below is a sample exam question and a paragraph written in answer to this question. The paragraph contains an argument which attempts to answer the question. However, there is an error in the argument. Use your knowledge of this topic to identify the flaw in the argument.

> How accurate is it to say that patronage was mainly responsible for the promotion of the Boleyn and Dudley families in the years 1525–1588?

When Anne Boleyn became the King's mistress in 1527 she became a source of patronage. Ambitious men flocked to Anne in the hope of impressing her and thereby benefitting from her largesse. When she became Queen in 1533 she also had her own household. Anne's family became a source of patronage. Thomas Boleyn is a good example of a man made rich and powerful by virtue of his daughter's patronage. Powerful courtiers could establish networks of support in the kingdom. For example, in Elizabeth's reign, the Queen's favourite, Robert Dudley, Earl of Leicester, was in a position to rewards several hundred men who thus became his clients. This enabled Leicester to extend his influence and exercise royal authority in regions in which his client base was strongest.

Royal progresses beyond London and the Home Counties

Royal progresses were an integral part of the sovereign's routine. Although the Court and royal household were more firmly based in the royal palaces in and around London, they were flexible enough to be mobile. During the winter months the royal household tended to restrict their travel to those palaces located in and near London, or in the Thames valley. It was the summer months that witnessed the true royal progresses. Each year the monarch went on progress in order to see and be seen by the people.

Each year the royal household published an itinerary, along with the names of those courtiers who would be accompanying the monarch. The monarch travelled with such a large entourage that only the wealthiest landowners could afford to host the royal party. To save money, the monarch tended to visit and stay in the mansion houses of their most favoured courtiers. The courtiers were expected to foot the bill for the privilege of having the monarch stay with them. It is perhaps ironic given their later dissolution but Henry VIII also enjoyed staying at monastic houses whilst on progress. His favourite abbey was Reading but he also stayed at Tewkesbury and Abingdon.

Sir Nicholas Poyntz and the royal progress to Gloucestershire, 1535

When Sir Nicholas Poyntz of Iron Acton in Gloucestershire was informed that the King intended to visit his house in August 1535, he was determined to impress his sovereign. Poyntz employed over 350 labourers and spent nine months building a magnificent new East Wing on the existing moated manor house. He paid a small fortune, even though Henry and Anne Boleyn spent no more than three days at Iron Acton. Unsurprisingly, perhaps, Poyntz found himself heavily in debt in 1546, and he was taken to court for not paying his rents to the King!

Although the visit of the monarch was a sign of favour, it did not guarantee continued patronage. Within 10 years of the King's visit, Poyntz was no longer part of the King's 'inner circle' of favoured courtiers. In fact, he found himself in court on charges of assault, for which he spent some time in the King's prison.

Elizabethan progresses

Like her father and grandfather, Elizabeth enjoyed her summer progresses. She was aware of the need to show herself to her people, and to impress upon her subjects her power and authority. She tended to stay longer at some of her courtiers' houses. For example, in the summer of 1575 she spent nearly three weeks at the Earl of Leicester's home of Kenilworth Castle in Warwickshire. The visit almost bankrupted him. The costs involved in hosting the royal party could be enormous. For example, the mayor and civic dignitaries of Bristol spent over £1,000 (£149,000 today) hosting Elizabeth and her entourage on her visit in 1574. For the Bristol municipal authorities, the Queen's visit was regarded a privileged occasion, with an opportunity to strengthen ties to the Crown in the hope of gaining some royal patronage.

Simple essay style `a`

Below is a sample exam question. Use your own knowledge and the information on the opposite page to produce a plan for this question. Choose four general points and provide three pieces of specific information to support each general point. Once you have planned your essay, write the introduction and conclusion for the essay. The introduction should list the points to be discussed in the essay. The conclusion should summarise the key points and justify which point was the most important.

'The key factor in promoting and extending royal authority in the years 1485–1603 was the use of the royal progress.' How far do you agree with this statement?

Turning assertion into argument `a`

Below is a sample exam question and a series of assertions. Read the exam question and then add a justification to each of the assertions to turn it into an argument.

How far did the Crown succeed in extending and cementing its authority in the kingdom in the period between 1485 and 1603?

The Crown was successful in extending and cementing its authority in the kingdom because

_____

_____

The Crown was only partially successful in extending and cementing its authority in the kingdom because

_____

_____

In some respects the Crown's attempt to make its presence felt in the north of England was largely unsuccessful because

_____

_____

Exam focus

Below is a sample answer on the events connected with the problem of poverty and vagrancy and the Crown's relationship with the localities.

'The most significant action taken by Tudor governments (1485–1603) to gain the co-operation of the localities was in dealing with the problem of poverty and vagrancy.' How far do you agree with this statement?

The period between 1485 and 1603 witnessed a concerted effort by successive Tudor governments to extend the power of the Crown into the localities. One way in which it attempted to do this was by assisting local authorities to deal with the potentially serious problems of poverty and vagrancy. The 'terror of the tramp' was a well-known phenomenon in the Tudor period. People were frightened by the rising tide of crime caused by what they perceived to be growing numbers of masterless men roaming the countryside. By promoting and enforcing parliamentary laws and royal proclamations, the Crown and central government sought to extend its influence and authority in those regions hit particularly hard by high levels of poverty and crime.

Tudor governments had been actively dealing with poverty and vagrancy for much of the period, though they had little understanding of the causes. As early as 1495 Henry VII's government tried to legislate the problem out of existence. The Vagrancy Act was intended to deter begging by issuing harsh punishments for those who ignored the law. It did nothing to solve the problem. The next Act was passed by Henry VIII in 1531, which tried to deal with vagrants in the same harsh way. However, there was some change in attitudes, as the poor were divided into the deserving and undeserving poor. The deserving poor got relief but the undeserving got punishment. Thereafter the passing of Tudor poor laws occurred more regularly because the problem got worse. The harshest legislation was passed in 1547 by Edward VI and is nicknamed the 'Slavery Act' because it condemned regular law breakers to serve a two-year period of slavery working for the state.

It took until the reign of Elizabeth before the government seriously tried to investigate and understand the problems of poverty and vagrancy. The system of poor relief was based in the parishes and not administered centrally. In the local parish system, four overseers were appointed in each parish to supervise the administration of poor relief. These overseers were responsible for finding apprenticeships for parish children and employment for able-bodied adults. The aim was to prevent able-bodied men roaming the countryside, even though many of them were simply searching for work. To help the deserving poor, parishes were empowered to build hospitals for the old, the sick and the disabled. Each parish was to pay a compulsory poor rate but the poorer parishes with a large number of paupers could be subsidised by richer parishes. Until the reign of Elizabeth, the state was not involved in any funding.

On the other hand, it could be argued that dealing with the problem of poverty and vagrancy was not the most significant action taken by Tudor governments. The system of poor relief had been developing gradually since the first act in Henry VIII's reign and it continued haphazardly into Edward VI's reign, until it reached its natural conclusion with the passing of the 1601 Poor Law. This Poor Law remained in place until 1834.

There are other equally important examples of significant action taken by Tudor governments in the localities. For example, the Tudor subsidy in 1513, which combined a tax on rank for the nobility with an income tax on property and income for commoners in the localities, was a government measure that had a significant impact on taxpayers in the localities because it was regarded as a fairer way of raising money than blanket subsidies.

This is a reasonably focused introduction that provides some context to the question.

This paragraph attempts to deal with the statement that the most significant action taken by Tudor governments to gain the co-operation of the localities was in dealing with the problem of poverty and vagrancy.

This paragraph further explores the statement and offers a list-like explanation with a one-line judgement to round it off.

This paragraph provides the counter-argument, based on the premise that dealing with the problem of poverty and vagrancy was not the most significant action taken by Tudor governments to involve themselves in the localities.

This paragraph is another more obvious list-like approach to the question. The points are relevant but not debated. This is mainly description.

The impact on the localities of the Statute of Artificers in 1563, whereby local magistrates had the responsibility of fixing prices and imposing maximum wages, was a highly significant action. The increasing importance of the role of Justices of the Peace throughout the whole period, dating back to the reign of Henry VII, was also significant because it enabled Tudor central government to transmit its orders directly to local authorities.

On balance, one might argue that the quotation is correct and that most significant action taken by Tudor governments to gain the co-operation of the localities was in dealing with the problem of poverty and vagrancy.

The candidate fails to offer a balanced conclusion and merely agrees with the statement.

This is a satisfactory essay. The range of issues identified and supported in this answer demonstrates a satisfactory level of appropriate knowledge. The premise of the question is not always addressed throughout, with a limited attempt to evaluate by exploring the counter-argument. There is a weak attempt to reach a judgement, more could have been done to develop the counter-argument and the conclusion is far too brief.

Identify the structure

It is not only important to develop an accurate written style but also useful to practise how to structure an answer. Identify the pattern in this answer by counting the sentences in each paragraph. It is also important to include some supporting information. Look at the second, third or fourth paragraphs and highlight the supporting information that is used to develop each explanation.

Timeline

1485   Henry VII's accession to the throne after victory at the battle of Bosworth

1487   Battle of Stoke, ending the Wars of the Roses; Lambert Simnel captured

1489   Yorkshire Rebellion

1497   Cornish Rebellion; Truce of Ayton

1499   Execution of the Pretender, Perkin Warbeck and Edward, Earl of Warwick

1509   Death of Henry VII; Henry VIII inherits the throne

1511–12   First French War

1513   Subsidy drawn up by Wolsey

1515   Wolsey made a cardinal (November) and appointed Lord Chancellor (December)

1518   Wolsey appointed papal legate

1521   Henry VIII given title of Defender of the Faith by the Pope

1525   Amicable Grant

1526   Eltham Ordinances

1529   Wolsey falls from power; meeting of the Reformation Parliament

1530   Thomas More becomes Lord Chancellor

1532   More resigns as Lord Chancellor; Thomas Cromwell becomes the King's chief adviser.

1533   Thomas Cranmer becomes Archbishop of Canterbury

1534   Act of Supremacy passed, severing England's ties with Rome and making Henry VIII head of the Church in England

1536   First Act for the dissolution of the monasteries passed in parliament; Pilgrimage of Grace rebellion breaks out in northern England; Act of Ten Articles; First Act of Union

1540   Second Act for the dissolution of the monasteries passed in parliament; execution of Cromwell

1543   Second Act of Union

1547   Death of Henry VIII; succeeded by Edward VI; government headed by Lord Protector Somerset

1549   Dissolution of the chantries; the Western Rebellion (Prayer Book Rebellion) and Kett's Rebellion break out; Somerset replaced as head of government by Lord President Northumberland; First Book of Common Prayer drawn up and published by Archbishop Cranmer

1552   Second Book of Common Prayer published

1553   Death of Edward VI; succeeded by Mary I after the defeat of the Lady Jane Grey conspiracy

1554   Wyatt Rebellion; execution of Northumberland and Lady Jane Grey

1555   Mary restores the Pope as head of the Church

1556   Execution of Archbishop Cranmer; Cardinal Reginald Pole appointed Archbishop of Canterbury

1558   Death of Mary; succeeded by Elizabeth I

1559   Church Settlement; Acts of Supremacy and Uniformity

1563   Statute of Artificers

1568   Mary, Queen of Scots, arrives in England following civil war in Scotland; she is immediately detained

1569   Rebellion of the Northern Earls (Northern Rebellion)

1570   Elizabeth excommunicated by the Pope; terms of the Act of Uniformity enforced

1587   Mary, Queen of Scots, executed

1588   Spanish Armada

1594   Outbreak of Nine Years' War

1598   Lord Burghley dies and is succeeded as chief minister by his son Sir Robert Cecil; Act for the Relief of the Poor

1601   Essex Rebellion; execution of Essex; Act for the Relief of the Poor

1603   Death of Elizabeth I; end of Nine Years' War

  Quick quizzes at **www.hoddereducation.co.uk/myrevisionnotes**

Glossary

Act of Supremacy   Act passed through parliament in 1534 recognising Henry VIII as head of the Church in England. Another Act was passed in 1559, by which Elizabeth became Supreme Governor of the Church.

Act of Uniformity   Act passed through parliament enforcing religious conformity.

Acts of Union   Acts passed through parliament uniting Wales with England politically, legally and administratively.

Annul   To cancel or invalidate.

Attainder   To confiscate the goods and property of a person found guilty of treason.

Barony   Name given to land ruled by a baron, a member of the nobility.

Bondmen   Servants who live and work on a lord's landholding and are tied by contract to serve their employer.

Borough and county constituencies   Urban and rural areas with the right to elect representatives to parliament.

Bosworth   Battle fought in Leicestershire on 22 August 1485 between the Lancastrian claimant, Henry Tudor, and the Yorkist king, Richard III.

Carthusian   Religious order of monks.

Church Settlement   Also known as the Elizabethan Church Settlement. Acts passed through parliament, setting up the Anglican Church and rules of worship.

Clan   Large extended family group tied by kinship and united by social, economic and political aims.

Comperta Monastica   Document drawn up by Cromwell to question and record the behaviour of monks and nuns.

Convocation   Term used to describe the ruling council of the Church, a form of parliament.

Council of the North   Council of ministers led by a president based in York, with the power to govern the north of England on behalf of the Crown.

County Palatine   Secular and/or ecclesiastical lordships ruled by noblemen or bishops, possessing special authority and autonomy from the rest of a kingdom.

Court of the King's Bench   Senior criminal court based in London.

Courts of Assize   Senior courts held in each county presided over by a judge appointed by the Crown.

Debasement of the coinage   Means whereby the government tried to save money by reducing the content of gold and silver in coins and replacing them with cheaper metals, such as copper, which lowered the value of the currency.

Edwardian Prayer Book   Protestant Prayer Book used in Church services. It was issued with amendments in 1549 and 1552.

Eltham Ordinances   Wolsey's attempt to reform the King's household in 1526.

Enclosure   Enclosing of land with hedges or fences to make it easier to raise livestock.

Excommunicate   To expel or banish a person from the Church. An excommunicant could no longer worship, marry or be buried in a church.

Forty-two Articles   Drawn up by Thomas Cranmer as a summary of Anglican doctrine in the Protestant faith in the reign of Edward VI.

Franciscans   Religious order of monks.

Great Chain of Being   Social pyramid showing everyone's place in society as decreed by God.

Heretics   Religious nonconformists who reject the teachings and rules of the Catholic Church.

Holy Roman Empire   Large, central European state, roughly equivalent to modern Germany, ruled by an elected emperor.

Humanism   European movement concerned with intellectual, educational, philosophical and religious learning and writing.

Hundred Years War   War fought in France between England and France in the years 1338–1453.

Justice of the Peace (JP)   Royal officer responsible for government, administration and justice at county level.

King's Council   Council consisting of the King's closest advisers.

King-and-parliament and king-in-parliament   Integration of two important institutions – the Crown and Parliament – in the 1530s.

King's writ did not run   The King's written orders were not recognised and had no force in law.

Lancastrians   Political group consisting of noblemen who supported the claim of the House of Lancaster to the English throne.

Lord Chancellor   Highest legal and administrative office in the English government, often equated with the monarch's chief minister.

Lord Deputy   Royally appointed governor of Ireland, who ruled through a council of ministers based in Dublin.

Lord Protector   Legal title given to senior nobleman appointed to govern the kingdom on behalf of a child monarch.

Lordship   Name given to a territory ruled by a lord or baron.

Lord Lieutenant   Military officer appointed to a county, concerned with the training of troops and the defence of the realm.

Lutheran   Followers of Martin Luther.

Marcher lordships   Semi-independent lordships in Wales and the border region, ruled by noblemen possessing special authority from the Crown.

Martial law   Short-term emergency law which supersedes a nation's traditional laws.

Mercenaries   Professional troops for hire.

Monopoly   Means of rewarding courtiers by granting them licences to collect tax or import duties on such commodities as starch, sugar and wine.

Papal Bull   Act passed by a Pope, issued to specific countries as a legally binding document.

Papal primacy   Power of the Pope in spiritual matters affecting the Roman Catholic Church in Europe.

Pilgrimage of Grace   Rebellion in the north of England in 1536–37.

Political nation   Wealthy, educated landowning elite wielding political power in the kingdom and dominating its parliament.

Pontefract Articles   List of grievances and demands drawn up by Robert Aske during the Pilgrimage of Grace.

Privy councillors   Senior government ministers who met with and advised the monarch in a private ruling council. They managed the government of the kingdom on behalf of the monarch.

Prorogue   Temporary suspension of parliament.

Puritan movement   Radical Protestants who reject all Catholic practices in church worship.

Quarter Sessions   Courts held four times a year in every county and presided over by JPs.

Recusants   Catholics in Elizabethan England who remained loyal to the Pope and refused to conform to the state religion.

Reformation Parliament   The parliament that met between 1529 and 1536 and transformed the Church by breaking from Rome and making Henry VIII Supreme Head of the Church in England.

Regular clergy   Monks and nuns who lived and worshipped in monastic institutions.

Renaissance   Flowering of knowledge in the late fifteenth and sixteenth centuries, focusing on science, art and the study of classical civilisation.

Royal prerogative   Rights and privileges that traditionally belonged to the monarch, such as making war and peace and marriage.

Scorched-earth tactics   Policy designed to deny an invading army food or shelter by destroying buildings and crops.

Sheriff   Local law official, akin to a police officer, working within each county.

Statute of Artificers   Act of parliament that sought to fix prices, regulate wages, restrict workers' freedom of movement and promote training.

Subsidy Act, 1513   Wolsey's attempt to raise money to pay for the war in France by assessing the value of a person's goods.

Thirty-Nine Articles   Defining statements of doctrine of the Church of England, setting out acts of worship in church services in the reign of Elizabeth I.

Valor Ecclesiasticus   Document drawn up by Cromwell to record the wealth and general financial status of monasteries in England and Wales.

Vicegerent   Office created by Henry VIII for Thomas Cromwell, empowering him to govern the Church on behalf of the Crown.

Yeomen   Social class of richer peasants who may have been as wealthy as some of the gentry but were below them in social class.

Yorkists   Political group consisting of noblemen who supported the claim of the House of York to the English throne.

Key figures

Robert Aske (d.1537)   Lawyer from Yorkshire who led the rebellion known as the Pilgrimage of Grace.

Sir Henry Bagenal (d.1598)   English landowner in Ireland and commander of English forces tasked to deal with the Irish rebellion. He was killed in battle.

Sir Francis Bigod (d.1537)   Northern landowner who rebelled after the Pilgrimage of Grace ended. His rebellion failed and he was executed.

Charles Blount, Lord Mountjoy (d.1606)   Lord Deputy of Ireland and commander of English forces in southern Ireland. He won the battle at Kinsale against the Spanish and Irish rebel forces commandeered by Tyrone.

Anne Boleyn (d.1536)   Second wife of Henry VIII, faction leader and one of the main causes of the break with Rome.

Margaret of Burgundy (d.1503)   Sister of Edward IV and Richard III and key supporter of the Yorkists. Funded and supported the Pretenders Simnel and Warbeck.

Catherine of Aragon (d.1536)   Daughter of Ferdinand and Isabella of Spain. Married Henry VII's son Prince Arthur in 1501, but following his death she married Henry VIII in 1509.

William Cecil, Lord Burghley (d.1598)   Secretary of State in Edward VI's reign and chief minister during the reign of Elizabeth. He was one of the most powerful men in English politics.

Charles VIII (d.1498)   King of France who supported Henry VII's invasion of England. He went to war with Henry VII in 1491 but agreed to a lasting peace in the Treaty of Étaples 1492.

Thomas Cranmer (d.1556)   Cleric and scholar who became Archbishop of Canterbury. He led the Reformation in England but was executed for his Protestant faith by Mary I.

Thomas Cromwell (d.1540)   Trained lawyer who served Cardinal Wolsey as his chief adviser and then Henry VIII as his chief minister.

Edmund Dudley (d.1510)   Minister responsible for tax collection in Henry VII's government, who was executed by Henry VIII.

John Dudley, Duke of Northumberland (d.1554)   Son of Edmund Dudley, Henry VII's adviser. He became Lord President of the Council and ruled England on behalf of Edward VI from 1549–53. He was executed by Queen Mary.

Robert Dudley, Earl of Leicester (d.1588)   Son of John Dudley, Duke of Northumberland, Dudley became one of Elizabeth's closest friends and adviser. He was a member of the Privy Council and one of the most influential men in English politics.

Robert Devereux, Earl of Essex (d.1601)   One of Queen Elizabeth's favourites, powerful at Court. His expedition to Ireland was criticised. He rebelled against the Queen in 1601 and was executed.

Edward, Earl of Warwick (d.1499)   Nephew of Edward IV and Richard III who was kept as a prisoner as a child. He was executed, years later, for plotting with Warbeck against Henry VII.

John Fisher (d.1535)   English bishop and humanist scholar who opposed Henry VIII's annulment, his marriage with Anne Boleyn and the break with Rome. He was executed in 1535.

Stephen Gardiner (d.1555)   English bishop who led the conservative faction at court during the reigns of Henry VIII and Edward VI. He was imprisoned by Edward VI but released by Mary I, whom he served as a minister in her government.

Thomas Howard, Duke of Norfolk (d.1554)   Powerful nobleman who served on Henry VIII's council and led the conservative faction at court. Retired from politics during Edward VI's reign but served on Mary's council.

Robert Kett (d.1549)   Landowner and tanner from Norfolk. Led the biggest rebellion of Edward VI's reign. After its failure he was executed.

Florence MacCarthy (d.1640)   Clan leader in Ireland. He was a skilled military man who joined the Irish rebellion late but managed to avoid execution by making peace with the English.

Thomas More (d.1535)   Lawyer and humanist scholar who became Henry VIII's Lord Chancellor in 1530. He resigned in 1532 and refused to accept Henry as head of the Church, for which he was executed.

Hugh Roe O'Donnell (d.1602)   Powerful clan leader in Ireland. He was a gifted military tactician and initially led the Irish rebellion, until Tyrone joined and took over the leadership.

Hugh O'Neill, Earl of Tyrone (d.1616)   Largest landowner and the most powerful man in Ulster. He was educated and trained in military matters in England but rebelled against Elizabeth to maintain his independence.

John de la Pole, Earl of Lincoln (d.1487) Nephew of Edward IV and Richard III. He was a leader of the Yorkists after the death of Richard III. He was killed at the battle of Stoke.

Sir Edward Poynings (d.1521) Soldier, administrator and diplomat. He was appointed to his highest office as Lord Deputy of Ireland by Henry VII.

Edward Seymour, Duke of Somerset (d.1552) Brother of Jane Seymour, wife of Henry VIII and uncle of Edward VI. He ruled England as Lord Protector from 1547–49, but was removed from power by John Dudley.

Lambert Simnel (d.1535) Impostor who pretended to be the nephew of Edward IV. He was a figurehead for dissident Yorkists seeking to topple Henry VII. He was pardoned and served in the King's household.

Perkin Warbeck (d.1499) Impostor who pretended to be the younger son of Edward IV. He was a figurehead for dissident Yorkists seeking to topple Henry VII.

Thomas Wolsey (d.1530) Powerful churchman who held various offices in Church and state. He was Henry VIII's chief minister for around 15 years.

Mark schemes

For some of the activities in the book it will be useful to refer to the mark scheme. Paper 3 requires two mark schemes, one for the AO1 assessments in Sections B and C, and another for Sections A's AO2 assessment.

AO1 mark scheme

- **Analytical focus**
- **Accurate detail**
- **Supported judgement**
- **Argument and structure**

	Marks
Level 1 ● Simplistic, limited focus ● Limited detail, limited accuracy ● No judgement or asserted judgement ● **Limited organisation, no argument**	1-3
Level 2 ● Descriptive, implicit focus ● Limited detail, mostly accurate ● Judgement with limited support ● **Basic organisation, limited argument**	4–7
Level 3 ● Some analysis, clear focus (may be descriptive in places) ● Some detail, mostly accurate ● Judgement with some support, based on implicit criteria ● **Some organisation, the argument is broadly clear**	11–16
Level 4 ● Clear analysis, clear focus (may be uneven) ● Sufficient detail, mostly accurate ● Judgement with some support, based on valid criteria ● **Generally well organised, logical argument (may lack precision)**	13–16
Level 5 ● Sustained analysis, clear focus ● Sufficient accurate detail, fully answers the question ● Judgement with full support, based on valid criteria (considers relative significance) ● **Well organised, logical argument communicated with precision**	17–20

AO2 mark scheme

- Analytical focus
- Accurate detail
- Supported judgement

Level	Marks	Description
1	1–3	• Surface-level comprehension of the source, demonstrated by quoting or paraphrasing, without analysis. • Some relevant knowledge of the historical context is included, but links to the source are limited. • Either no overall evaluation of the source, or discussion of reliability and utility is very basic.
2	4–7	• Some understanding of the source, demonstrated by selecting and summarising relevant information. • Some relevant knowledge of the historical context is added to the source to support of challenge the detail it includes. • An overall judgement is presented, but with limited support. Discussions of reliability and utility are based on a limited discussion of provenance and may reflect invalid assumptions.
3	8–12	• Understanding of the source, demonstrated by some analysis of key points, explaining their meaning and valid inferences. • Relevant knowledge of the historical context is used to support inferences. Contextual knowledge is also used to expand on, support or challenge matters of detail from the source. • An overall judgement is presented, which relates to the nature and purpose of the source. The judgement is based on valid criteria, but the support is likely to be limited.
4	13–16	• Analysis of the source, demonstrated by examining their evidence to make reasoned inferences. Valid distinctions are made between information and opinion. Treatment of the two enquiries may be uneven. • Relevant knowledge of the historical context is used to reveal and discuss the limitations of the source's content. The answer attempts to interpret the source material in the context of the values and assumptions of the society it comes from. • Evaluation of the sources reflects how much weight the evidence of the sources can bear. Evaluation is based on valid criteria. Aspects of the judgement may have limited support.
5	17–20	• Confident interrogation of the source, in relation to both enquiries, demonstrated by reasoned inferences. The answer shows a range of ways the source can be used. Valid distinctions are made between information and opinion. • Relevant knowledge of the historical context is used to reveal and discuss the limitations of the source's content. The answer interprets the source material in the context of the values and assumptions of the society it comes from. • Evaluation of the source reflects how much weight the evidence of the source can bear and may distinguish between the degrees to which aspects of the sources can be useful. Evaluation is based on valid criteria.

Answers

Page 7, Spot the mistake

This does not get to a Level 4 because the answer is too simplistic – 'his father was an earl and not a king' or 'His grandfather was not even an Englishman; he was a Welsh squire' – and not fully focused on the key part of the question: 'to what extent'. The answer should offer a counter-argument by highlighting the strengths of Henry's claims to the throne.

Page 9, Support or challenge?

The following statement supports:

- The Pope and the King of Spain recognised his kingship

The following statements challenge:
- Henry dated his reign from the day before Bosworth
- Henry was victorious at the battle of Bosworth
- The birth of a son and heir established the dynasty
- Henry controlled the nobility
- Warwick was executed in 1499
- Henry successfully dealt with the Yorkist factions
- Margaret of Burgundy plotted against Henry VII

Page 9, Eliminate irrelevance

In some respects it is fair to say that Henry VII's prospects of holding on to his throne improved significantly after the birth of Prince Arthur. ~~Henry deliberately chose the name Arthur to impress his subjects because it linked the Tudor dynasty to a glorious past.~~ Securing a son and heir may have convinced his subjects that he was here to stay and that the dynasty was likely to survive. ~~Richard III did not have a son and heir so he was forced to nominate his nephew John de la Pole as his successor.~~ The fact that Arthur was the son of Henry of Richmond and Elizabeth of York did much to unite the Lancastrian and Yorkist factions. Arthur's birth symbolised the union of York and Lancaster and helped end the dynastic conflict ~~that had dominated English politics in the 30 years before Henry VII's accession in 1485.~~

(The statements are merely description and do not specifically address the question.)

Page 11, Spectrum of importance

Most important:
- 4 The death of the Earl of Lincoln at Stoke
- 2 Victory in battle is seen as a sign of God's support
- 6 Victory in battle enhances Henry VII's reputation

Least important:
- 5 Simnel is pardoned and employed in the King's service
- 1 Warbeck's capture and execution

- 3 The French King abandons Warbeck

Page 13, Write the question

Assess the value of the source for revealing the attitude of the Spanish to the Pretender Warbeck and why the Spanish were concerned by the close relationship between the French and the Holy Roman Empire.

Page 15, Complete the paragraph

Overall, Henry's foreign policy can be regarded as a success because he was never seriously threatened and he remained King until his death from natural causes.

Page 17, Simple essay style

Point 1: Scotland's threat
- Scotland was England's traditional enemy with a long history of conflict.
- The Scots had a long-standing alliance with the French.
- The Scots shared a land border with England which made the latter vulnerable to invasion.

Point 2: Scotland's weaknesses
- The Scots were financially and militarily weaker than the English.
- The Scots could be bought off for the right price.
- The French only became involved in Scottish affairs when it suited their purpose.

Point 3: Burgundy's threat
- Margaret of Burgundy was a formidable enemy and consistent in her opposition to Henry.
- Burgundy had the financial resources to fund rebellions and pretenders and provide mercenary troops.
- Burgundy could hurt England economically by stopping the lucrative English cloth trade.

Point 4: Burgundy's weaknesses
- Burgundy was alone among the European nations to oppose Henry VII
- Burgundy failed to create an alliance of powerful European nations against Henry VII
- Burgundy's support was largely limited to finance

Introduction: list the points to be discussed in the essay, e.g. Scotland's threat and its weaknesses, Burgundy's threat and weaknesses.

Conclusion: summarise the key points and justify which point was the most important.

Page 21, Complete the paragraph

Overall, Henry's desire to secure the succession was mainly responsible for the Royal Supremacy because the King needed a male heir to succeed him and only an annulment of his barren marriage could enable him to marry Anne Boleyn, who he believed would provide him with a son.

Page 23, Develop the detail

When Henry VIII assumed the title of Supreme Head of the Church the monasteries were doomed. The King's title and his supremacy were engineered by Thomas Cromwell, a Lutheran sympathiser and enemy of the monastic vocation. He was determined to impress the King by finding evidence of wrongdoing which would enable him to destroy the monasteries and thereby exploit their wealth. The *Valor Ecclesiasticus* provided Cromwell with the material he needed to convince the King that the dissolution was not only the right thing to do, it was necessary.

When Henry VIII assumed the title supreme head of the church **the monasteries were doomed**.

Additional detail: Henry did not trust the monasteries or some of the abbots who led them. Henry saw them as a potential threat, covert supporters of the Pope and likely to oppose his leadership of the church.

The King's title and his supremacy were engineered by Thomas Cromwell, a **Lutheran sympathiser and enemy of the monastic vocation**.

Additional detail: As a matter of principle Protestants rejected the monastic way of life.

The *Valor Ecclesiasticus* **provided Cromwell with the material he needed to convince the King that the dissolution was not only the right thing to do, it was necessary**.

Additional detail: The *Valor* provided a comprehensive analysis of the wealth of the monasteries. This, coupled with the evidence of clerical corruption and wrongdoing, enabled Cromwell to make a strong case to convince a sceptical King that all monasteries could and should be dissolved.

Page 25, Identify an argument

The first conclusion is mainly description and assertion.

Description: For example:

- First, there was the work of Cromwell's commissioners who went around the northern counties surveying the wealth of the Church.

Assertion: For example:
- They were distrusted and disliked by the people.
- Cromwell too was hated and blamed for persuading the King to consider imposing these taxes.

Northerners tended to resent southerners interfering in their affairs so they believed the rumours. The rumours that the monasteries were going to be closed were not as important to the people because the proposed taxation on baptisms, marriage and funerals affected them directly.

The second conclusion would gain a higher mark because it contains reason and argument.

Reason: For example:
- This is why the Tudors passed laws against people spreading unfounded rumours.
- People were determined to defend their Church and their religious way of life so a tax on such fundamental activities as baptism, marriage and funerals made the population angry because they could not be avoided.

Argument: For example:
- The key feature here is the word 'rumour', because in a world without the technology to broadcast news, information was transmitted by word of mouth or by written and oral proclamation.
- To suggest that rumours of a tax on baptisms, marriage and funerals were mainly responsible for the outbreak of rebellion is perhaps going too far. There were other equally significant causes of rebellion such as the closure of the monasteries – another action stimulated by rumour – and the more tangible, and visible, work of Cromwell's commissioners in visiting parish churches and local monasteries.

Page 27, Turning assertion into argument

The Pilgrimage of Grace posed a significant challenge because **of its sheer size in the numbers taking part and because of the geographical extent of the uprising.**

The Pilgrimage of Grace did not pose a significant challenge because **many of those who took part in the uprising were not trained soldiers and they would likely have fled at the first sign of professional troops being sent against them.**

The example set by the rebels in the Pilgrimage of Grace was serious because **it might have encouraged other regions of England to rise up against the Crown.**

The Pilgrimage of Grace can be seen as merely a protest movement which supported rather than opposed Henry VIII and his government **because the rebels blamed the King's chief minister, Thomas Cromwell, rather than the divinely ordained monarch.**

Page 29, Support your judgement

Overall, Henry did more than most to suppress the rebellions because the final decision rested with him **and it was the King who met with and made promises** to the rebel leaders. **He alone had the confidence and conviction to persuade the rebels to disperse and go home.**

Generally, Henry VIII's success in suppressing the rebellious north owed as much to Cromwell and Norfolk as to his own efforts **for although the final decision rested with Henry he relied on the advice of men such as Cromwell. Henry also relied on men like Norfolk to carry out his orders.**

Page 31, Establish criteria

Definition: Mistakes made by the rebels that contributed to the failure of their rebellion.

Criteria:
- Trust
- Divine right of kings
- Hasty dispersal of the rebels
- Bigod's rebellion

Page 35, Spectrum of importance

Most important:
- 1 Policy and impact of the enclosing of land
- 3 Social turmoil and economic difficulties
- 2 Somerset's weakness as a ruler

Least important:
- 4 Decline and depression in the cloth trade
- 5 The Vagrancy Act
- 6 Breakdown in the notion and principles of the Great Chain of Being

Page 37, Develop the detail

Between 1547 and 1549 Somerset's government did not succeed in solving the **problems associated with high inflation and rising unemployment.** Somerset's policies were aimed at **promoting arable farming as opposed to the less labour-intensive pastoral farming**. He hoped this would reduce unemployment and bring down inflation. However, he had failed to fully appreciate the scale of the kingdom's social and economic problems which is why his policy on enclosure was unlikely to work. Overall, it is clear that Somerset did not understand the problems and nor did he have a credible plan to solve them.

Page 39, Simple essay style

Point 1: Landlords
- Motivated by profit
- Rise in rents and in 'rack-renting'
- Increased enclosure of common land.

Point 2: Kett's Rebellion
- Anger at unsympathetic attitude of landowner Sir John Flowerdew
- Evidence of cruel and unsympathetic landlords was sufficient to provide Kett with effective propaganda

- Size of rebellion – 16,000 strong – is evidence of widespread anger and dissatisfaction.

Point 3: Protesters and rebels
- Troublemakers simply out to cause trouble
- High inflation, rising food prices and unemployment
- Perceived lack of sympathy on part of authorities and Church leaders.

Point 4: Western rebellion
- Anger at religious changes and promotion of Protestantism
- Resentment at dissolution of the chantries
- Unhappy with translation of and enforced use of English Prayer Book.

Introduction: list the points to be discussed in the essay, e.g. landlords, Kett's Rebellion, protesters and rebels, Western rebellion.

Conclusion: summarise the key points and justify which point was the most important.

Page 41, Qualify your judgement

The best judgment about the value of Source 1 is that contained in point 3 because it provides a balanced judgement about the quality of Kett's leadership and the reason why he was defeated.

Page 43, Select the detail

Somerset did not listen to the advice of his Council – '**I told your Grace the truth and was not believed'.**

Somerset's rule was weak – **'your softness, your intention to be good, your gentleness'.**

Source 1 is valuable to a historian for revealing the privy councillors' attitudes towards Somerset's rule, and the condition of England in 1549 because **it reveals the groundswell of opposition that was rising from within the government against Somerset.**

Page 45, Establish criteria

Definition: Failure to lead effectively or to organise efficiently, failure to inspire or command respect, failure to plan or devise successful tactical strategy

Criteria:
- failure to lead effectively or to organise efficiently
- failure to inspire or command respect
- failure to plan or devise successful tactical strategy.

Page 49, You're the examiner

Level: 4; Mark: 20

Reason for choosing this level and this mark: The answer clearly answers the question set and is well supported by relevant and focused comments. The answer is well written and confident, and has an air of conviction.

Page 51, Moving from assertion to argument

The detention of Mary, Queen of Scots, in 1568 contributed to the outbreak of the Northern Rebellion because **it angered the Catholic nobility of Northern England.**

Mary, Queen of Scots' detention by Elizabeth I in 1568 caused some Catholic nobles to rebel in the north of England because **they resented the way in which an anointed Catholic Queen was being treated.**

Mary, Queen of Scots' detention by Elizabeth I in 1568 was only partially responsible for the outbreak of rebellion in the north of England because there were other equally significant factors that must be considered, such as the **personal ambitions of the Northern Earls.**

In many ways the detention of Mary, Queen of Scots, in 1568 was simply an excuse for already disaffected Catholic noblemen to vent their anger and frustration with the government by means of an armed insurrection **but this does not explain why it took them over ten years to rebel.**

Page 53, Develop the detail

Elizabeth was faced with an almost impossible decision when confronted with the reality of Mary Stuart's arrival on English soil: what should she do? Ignoring Mary was not an option, as the Scottish queen was now a resident in England and, as a former head of state, had to be dealt with according to her status. **There were a number of options available** to Elizabeth, all of which had been drawn up by her closest advisers. The first priority was to ensure Elizabeth's safety followed by a careful assessment of the threat posed by Mary.

Page 55, Developing an argument

The earls lacked the charisma needed to inspire men to rebel and follow their lead. They only managed to raise 6,000 men, which was simply not enough to confront a well-trained royal army. The early success they enjoyed at Durham filled them with confidence and encouraged them to believe that their rebellion was destined to succeed. **In fact, the ease with which the rebels took Durham lulled them into a false sense of their own power. They had become too complacent and blind to the dangers that lay ahead.**

However, instead of marching south in search of new recruits with the prospect of freeing Mary, Queen of Scots, the earls wasted time and resources. **They failed to grasp the seriousness of the situation and had underestimated the power of the Crown and its forces sent against them.** When the Crown did send an army against them, the rebels fled, which effectively

signalled the end of the revolt. **This bears all the hallmarks of poor leadership because they failed to achieve their aims partly because they failed to plan effectively.**

Page 57, Support your judgement

Overall, the rebellion failed because the earls were frightened into fleeing rather than engage in battle the royal army sent against them, **which suggests that they had little confidence of the ability of their followers to defeat the enemy.**

Generally, the Crown was able to impose itself on the rebels by threatening them, with superior armed force, **whereas the rebel forces were poorly led and did not command enough trained troops to confront the enemy.**

Page 63, Turning assertion into argument

Bagenal's ambition for land and power at the expense of the native Irish led to the Nine Years' War because **he represented the brutal face of English power in Ireland.**

Bagenal's personal antipathy for Tyrone was a significant cause of rebellion in Ulster because **it pushed a powerful, influential and hitherto loyal Irish nobleman into war.**

Bagenal was an ambitious man but he alone was not responsible for the Nine Years' War because **the tension between the native Irish and their English overlords had been brewing for nearly a century.**

In many ways Bagenal was as much a victim of the Crown's ambition for power in Ulster as Tyrone and O'Donnell **because the Crown was prepared to sacrifice friend and foe alike in its quest to fulfil its aims.**

Page 65, Establish criteria

Definition: defeat or humiliation with no means of recovery

Criteria:
- Defeat in battle
- Loss of pride and prestige
- Encouragement of further challenges to English power in Ireland

Page 67, Developing an argument

The Irish rebel commanders knew that to succeed they needed substantial support from abroad. Spain's diplomatic support was welcome but did not help them in their fight with the English in Ireland. A substantial Spanish army was needed if the Irish rebels were to defeat the English. The Spanish troops that did land in south-western Ireland did so unopposed but **the force was too small to have a significant impact on the rebellion. To make matters worse the Spanish commander failed to exploit the taking of Kinsale by remaining within the town.**

The Spanish expeditionary force needed immediate reinforcement if they were to challenge the English in a pitched battle. **The rebel Irish leaders were lulled into a false sense of security by the landing of Spanish troops in Ireland. Confident of success they moved too slowly, which explains why** Tyrone and O'Donnell arrived in Kinsale too late to do any good.

Page 69, Spot the inference

- Hugh O'Neill appeared to be reluctant to rebel against the English (I)
- The writer of Source 1 is taking more credit for the rebellion than he deserves (I)
- The Irish rebellion would fail without King Philip's help (X)
- The writer of Source 1 is undermining his brother's leadership of the rebellion (X)
- The rebel army consisted of outlaws, beggars and disgruntled exiled Irishmen (S)
- Hugh O' Neill could not be trusted because he planned the rebellion but did not lead it until later. Leaving others to fight the English (P)

Page 71, Spectrum of importance

Most important:
- 2 Bagenal was the most competent of the English battlefield commanders.
- 1 Mountjoy defeated the Irish rebels in battle.
- 6 Mountjoy's scorched-earth policy was cruel but effective in subduing the Irish.
- 3 Essex concluded a successful truce with the Irish rebel leader Hugh O'Neill.

Least important:
- 4 The Spanish army was too small and weak to threaten the English forces in Ireland.
- 5 Essex was a favourite of Queen Elizabeth.

Page 71, You're the examiner

Level: 3; Mark: 15

Reason for choosing this level and this mark: It is a well-written answer that focuses on the question set. However, it lacks balance because it does not address the other factors that contributed to Elizabeth's victory in the Nine Years' War. It needs to weigh up the relative strengths and weaknesses of all the factors that contributed to Elizabeth's victory.

Page 79, Spectrum of importance

Most important:
- 2 The Eltham Ordinances
- 3 The Tudor revolution in government
- 5 The role of the King
- 4 The Pilgrimage of Grace

Least important:
- 1 The King's Council
- 6 The Privy Council after Cromwell's death

Page 79, Developing an argument

There is no doubt that the system of government and administration underwent substantial change in the century after Henry VII's accession. **The King's Council had served the monarchy well but was outdated and in need of reform.** Henry VIII strengthened the machinery of government by approving the establishment of a Privy Council. The Council was responsible for passing such vital legislation as the union of Wales and England, which extended the reach and power of central government to the distant parts of the realm. The emergence of the Privy Council provided the government with a professional body capable of exercising authority over every aspect of Tudor administration. **This led to the development of ministerial responsibility, which evolved into the notion of collective responsibility. According to the late Professor G.R. Elton this re-organisation was part of Cromwell's grand scheme, a 'revolution in government' no less.**

Page 81, Simple essay style

Point 1: The contribution of Cecil
- Cecil inherited an office and extended its powers.
- During his tenure the office evolved into the Secretary of State.
- The office became synonymous with the role and duties of a chief minister.

Point 2: The contribution of Cromwell
- Cromwell began his rise to power as the principal secretary of Lord Chancellor Wolsey.
- Cromwell developed the office to become one of the offices of state during Henry VIII's reign.
- His tenure in power earned wider recognition for the office of the King's secretary.

Point 3: The minority of Edward VI
- Lord Protector Somerset continued the practice of employing a principal secretary.
- The most active secretary during the minority was a young William Cecil.
- The duties associated with a principal secretary was continued by Somerset's successor, Northumberland.

Point 4: The contribution of Wolsey and Henry VIII

- Wolsey first appointed Cromwell to be his secretary.
- Wolsey's employment of Cromwell came to the attention of the King.
- Henry VIII next employed Cromwell as his principal secretary.

Introduction: list the points to be discussed in the essay, e.g. the contribution of Cecil, the contribution of Cromwell, the minority of Edward VI and the contribution of Wolsey and Henry VIII.

Conclusion: summarise the key points and justify which point was the most important.

Page 83, Develop the detail

Between 1485 and 1603 the Lords Lieutenant succeeded in extending the power and authority of the Crown into the localities. They were able to do so because the offices were filled by powerful noblemen. These noble Lieutenants were wealthy landowners who wielded considerable influence. However, the primary role of the office of Lord Lieutenant was in military matters. The defence of the realm from possible invasion or internal rebellion was a matter of serious concern. Nevertheless, by virtue of their office the Lords Lieutenant were able to influence the running of local government and thereby promoting the power of the Crown.

Page 83, Turning assertion into argument

There were some significant changes in the role of the Lord Lieutenant in the second half of the sixteenth century because **of the need to defend the kingdom from possible invasion.**

The Crown's reforms led to a significant change in some aspects of the role of the Lord Lieutenant because **of the increased risk of invasion by Spain after war was declared in 1585.**

The Crown's reforms were only partial, and did not affect some fundamental aspects of the role of the Lord Lieutenant in the sense that **they did not directly govern the locality but merely supported the local Justices of the Peace who were responsible for the day-to-day running of the county.**

Page 87, Spot the mistake

There is no doubt that the status and authority of Parliament was significantly transformed in the years 1485–1603. In the reign of Henry VII parliament was a weak and insignificant institution but **by 1603 it had become more powerful than the Crown**. This was partly due to the fact that the monarch was a woman. **The Crown could not pass laws or raise revenue without the consent of parliament.**

'by 1603 it had become more powerful than the Crown'

Rewrite – it had attained a greater significance than before because of its ability to raise funds for the Crown.

'The Crown could not pass laws or raise revenue without the consent of Parliament.'

Rewrite – Although the Crown did not need the consent of Parliament to pass laws or raise revenue it was considered wise to involve MPs in the process so as to achieve a measure of consensus and stability.

Page 87, Identify key terms

Key word or term – permanent and essential

Key phrase – cause and impact

Brief essay plan:
- Parliament – nature, role and impact
- Other parts, roles and/or functions of royal government – the Crown, departments of state in central government such as the exchequer and chancery, regional councils and local government, the Privy Council
- Although parliament was making an increasingly essential contribution to the running of royal government, it had not become permanent.

Key word or term – important part

Key phrase – cause and impact.

Brief essay plan:
- Parliament – nature, role and impact
- Other parts, roles of royal government – the Crown, departments of state in central government such as the exchequer and chancery, regional councils and local government, the Privy Council
- In terms of parliament's ability to raise revenue it is accurate to say that it had become an important part of royal government by 1603.

Page 93, Simple essay style

Point 1: Royal policy
- To extend the power and authority of the Crown to the furthest parts of the kingdom
- To enhance the status and power of the monarch
- To control and exploit the revenues of the whole kingdom.

Point 2: Concept of a sovereign state
- It might be argued that this was part of Cromwell's revolution in government.
- The break with Rome eliminated any lingering foreign influence in English affairs.
- Church and state were unified.

Point 3: Local government in England
- The points of contact between central and local government were already in place, e.g. the Council of the North and the Council of Wales and the March.
- The Sheriff was the eyes and ears of the Crown.
- The Justices of the Peace were the willing servants of central government, especially the Privy Council.

Point 4: Lawlessness and disorder
- Wales was racked by lawlessness and disorder.
- The primary motive seems to have been to crush lawlessness and disorder and the potential for rebellion.
- Wales was only a small part of the kingdom.

Introduction: list the points to be discussed in the essay, e.g. royal policy, lawlessness and disorder, concept of a sovereign state and the contribution of Cromwell and Henry VIII.

Conclusion: summarise the key points and justify which point was the most important.

Page 93, Support your judgement
Overall, the Tudor Crown failed to create a stable and successful system of local government by 1603 **because it relied on the co-operation of powerful and influential noblemen who dominated local government in their capacity as Lord Lieutenants.**

Generally, Tudor monarchs were able to create a stable and successful system of regional and local government **by 1603 because it could rely on the willing cooperation of the local gentry who were happy to serve the Crown by filling the offices of justices of the peace in every county.**

Page 95, Identify the concept
'Grammar schools had little long-term impact on literacy levels among the yeomen farmers in the years 1485-1603.' How far do you agree with this statement? – Consequence

How far did borough representation in Parliament change in the years 1485–1603? – Change/continuity

How accurate is it to say that the years 1485-1603 witnessed a significant increase in merchants and lawyers being elected to Parliament? – Significance

How far do you agree that a wealthier yeoman class showed a greater awareness of and interest in politics, government and local office in the years 1485–1603? – Cause

Page 97, RAG – Rate the timeline
1485	Death of Richard III
1489	The Yorkshire rebellion
1513	Cardinal Wolsey's Subsidy
1533	Publication of Sir Thomas More's *Apologye*
1536	First Act of Union between Wales and England
1537	The Council of the North re-established
1543	Second Act of Union between Wales and England
1563	Statute of Artificers
1569	Rebellion of the Northern Earls
1586	Book of Orders

1598	Act for the Relief of the Poor
1601	Act for the Relief of the Poor
1603	Death of Elizabeth

Page 99, You're the examiner
Level 4, Mark 18

Reason for choosing this level and this mark: It is a well written and balanced conclusion that provides an analytical overview of the question set.

Page 101, Simple essay style
Point 1: Faction
- Boleyn and Norfolk factions
- Cromwell and Aragonese factions
- Cecil and Essex factions

Point 2: Patronage
- Competition for royal rewards
- Crown's ability to reward depended on a sound economy and solvent monarchy
- Crown's use of faction to divide and rule

Point 3: Faction conflicts other than patronage
- Boleyn and Norfolk factions fought Cromwell and Aragonese over the divorce and religion.
- Cecil and Essex factions fought over political power.
- Northumberland and Somerset fought over political power.

Point 4: The monarchs
- Henry VIII managed and controlled factions.
- Edward VI was too young to manage and control factions.
- Elizabeth controlled faction disputes until the last ten years of her reign.

Introduction: list the points to be discussed in the essay eg. faction, patronage, faction conflicts other than patronage and the monarchs.

Conclusion: summarise the key points and justify which point was the most important.

Page 103, Simple essay style
Point 1: Royal progress
- To extend the power and authority of the Crown to other parts of the kingdom
- To enhance the status and power of the monarch
- To allow the monarch to be seen by as many people as possible

Point 2: Developing the concept of the sovereign state
- Cromwell's revolution in government
- The break with Rome, which eliminated any lingering foreign influence in English affairs
- The unification of Church and state.

Point 3: Local government in England and Parliament

- The points of contact between central and local government were developed, e.g. the Council of the North and the Council of Wales and the March.
- The authority of the sheriff and justices of the peace was strengthened.
- Parliament was used as a means of gathering and reaching representatives from all parts of the kingdom.

Point 4: Central government and the power of the law courts

- Developing power of the King's Council and the later Privy Council
- The modernisation and professionalisation of central government department

- The power of the central law courts – Star Chamber, King's Bench, requests, Chancery and Exchequer – to extend the law into the furthest reaches of the kingdom.

Introduction: list the points to be discussed in the essay eg. Royal progress, developing the concept of the sovereign state and the contribution of Cromwell and Henry VIII

Conclusion: summarise the key points and justify which point was the most important.